MW01174266

STEPPING STONES

Stepping Stones

by Ellen Soo Sun Song Kang

HOLLYM
Elizabeth, NJ · Seoul

First published in 2003
by Hollym International Corp.
18 Donald Place, Elizabeth, New Jersey 07208, U.S.A.
Phone: (908) 353-1655   Fax: (908) 353-0255
http://www.hollym.com

Published simultaneously in Korea
by Hollym Corporation; Publishers
13-13 Gwancheol-dong, Jongno-gu, Seoul 110-111, Korea
Phone: (02) 735-7551~4   Fax: (02) 730-5149, 8192
http://www.hollym.co.kr e-mail: info@hollym.co.kr

ISBN: 1-56591-184-9
Library of Congress Control Number: 2003101450

Printed in Korea

| CHAPTERS |

| FORWORD |

Before retiring from an academic career in medicine, I resolved to write an account of my parents and our immediate family for our children to share with their own children. A narrative of our parents' immigration to the West was a logical starting point, but merely highlighting events and dates was never my intent. Furthermore, it soon became clear that I had to reach beyond my parents, touching on their own beginnings. Availability of immigration data through The Center for Korean Studies at the University of Hawaii allowed me to validate important dates on my parents, but data on their parents was unavailable to me. Consequently, I was pressed into another venue--inferring how things might have felt and been, imagining the motives behind moves or gestures that were made, and by surmise, rationalizing the underlying reasons that might have eventually motivated my parents to leave for the West. This approach depended on the recall of conversations overheard during my childhood and from shared understandings among my siblings. Admittedly, some license had to be taken to round out events and circumstances, here and there. However, such were drawn from my parents' innate natures, and habits and preferences as I perceived them, first as a child and later as an adult.

In this manner, I have sketched a sequence of plausible events that could lead a man and a woman, separately, to undertake a lonely odyssey to a foreign land where, while a change to a new life was a definite promise, the possibility of improving life must surely have been less certain.

I am grateful to each of my siblings, Evelyn, George, Henry, Andrew, and Jessica, for their helpful suggestions, but more importantly for their contributions to the stories recorded in "Stepping Stones". Thanks also to my patient and supportive husband, Andrew Ho Kang, and to each of my daughters, Cynthia, Edith, and Audrey, for their encouragement and helpful suggestions throughout the recording of this saga. Thanks to Mrs. Susan Postlethwaite, a dear friend, who made helpful suggestions after a reading of the first draft. I also want to thank my Editor, Ms. Julia Huijeong Yi of Hollym, who assisted me in the kindliest of ways.

Ellen Soo Sun Song Kang

Family Tree for Suk Soon Song and Bok Pil Chun

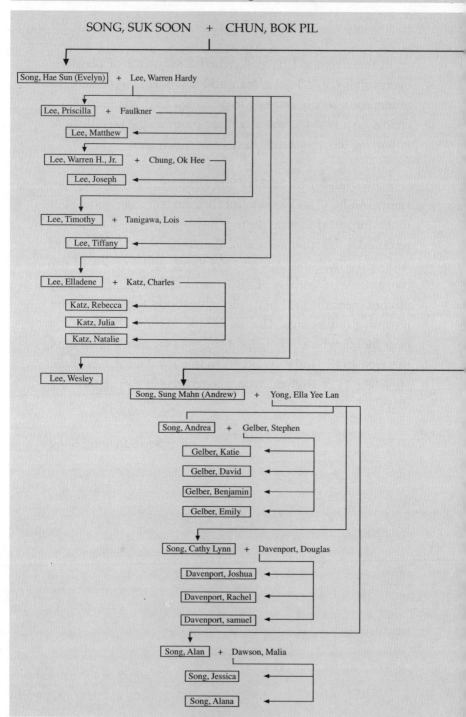

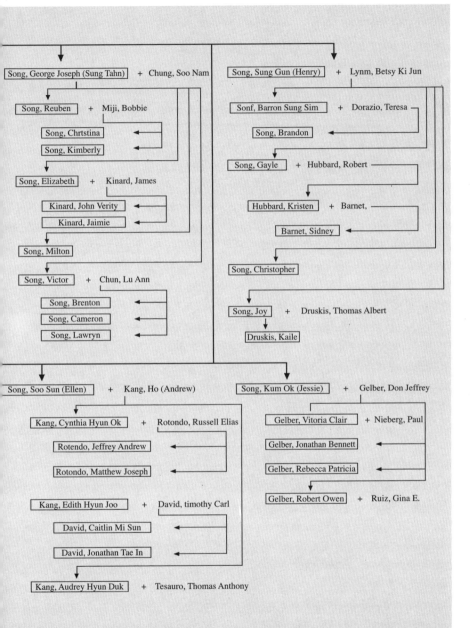

HONORABLE FATHER

Song, was past the fifth decade of life and naturally attributed the recent onset of morning stiffness and aches, where the bones met, to the consequences of aging. Of course, the never-ending, back-breaking work of tending the wet, terraced fields of rice as well as the other crops on drier, hard-to-till, rocky, stonier ground did not help, he admitted. He would endure he said to himself, as he rubbed his elbows, wrists and shoulders with his rough hands. Then arching backward, he stretched for a moment and then repeated these maneuvers again in the same sequence.

The ginseng root that he nibbled on during the day and the ground pine needle drink that his wife prepared for him each evening had not helped much. Because the rubbing and stretching brought immediate, though temporary relief, he regularly massaged his joints and stretched on arising each day.

He reached for the knotted hair fixed on top of his head. Sleep and the morning ritual had not displaced it. In fact, only a minor adjustment of the wooden stick holding the rolled up, greying bun of hair in a snug knot on top of his head was all that was necessary. He followed this with a swipe of his hand across his face, ending with a gentle tug at his pointed, thin, slightly greying beard.

He could hear his wife chanting softly outside beyond the veranda, as she stirred the contents of at least two brass pots simmering over the wood-burning stove made of piled-up rocks and stones daubed with clay.

She chanted, "Today, we hope for sunshine and rain. Sunshine until we complete our morning chores and rain thereafter." Her voice alternately trailed in a wailing tone, then trebled, before trembling and grasping for new words and phrases before repeating the same wish again.

It sounded like the chanting the Farmer heard in the village when they gathered for Chusok (harvest) celebrations. At that time, local players brought out their home-made instruments to celebrate the harvest. There was the stringed zither-like instrument that was plucked, another stringed piece that stood upright and was played with a bow, while the piri, a bamboo oboe, wailed and whined to the rhythmic but slow, syncopated beat of the hour-glass drum as it was beaten alternately with a stick and the drummer's hand.

She was actually singing a prayer to the one God, Hana-Nim (One Being) whom she and her family believed had control over the environment, the heavens, and all of the events of their lives. She was younger than he was and fortunately did not complain of bodily stiffness or aches and pains, as yet. Surely she would be spared the effects of aging, thought Song.

After breakfast each day, she would don her head piece, a cloth draped like a hood over her face at one end with the other end firmly tied under the hair bun at the back of the neck and proceed to help him with many of the lighter tasks in the fields. The kitchen duties were left to their daughter who was approaching a marriageable age, and their daughter-in-law, whenever her new baby was still.

While the hood shielded his wife's eyes from the direct rays of the sun and reduced the intensity of the heat, it failed to block the tanning and leathering effects of the sun on the exposed surfaces of her body. Tanned and leathered she bent over her cooking, interrupting her chanting only to give instructions to their daughter and daughter-in-law who were assisting her.

Soon the preparations for the largest meal of the day were completed. Upon the Farmer's return from the outside pit, his wife called out, "Achim-chap-sup-si-ooo!" (Breakfast is ready!)

The Farmer smiled and prepared to feast on the meal that was to sustain him through most of the working day. He sat on a flat pillow on the floor, his legs crossed and tucked under a small, low table set with bowls of rice and a soup made with cabbage, onion, tubu or tofu, and a fermented soy bean sauce flavored with garlic, the mainstays of breakfast each day. There were also small saucers filled with pickled roots, vegetables, and dried fish along with various spicy condiments to complement the meal. A cup of tea stood steaming on his right.

He reached for a porcelain spoon with one hand and bent his head towards the bowl of soup. Sucking deeply of the first spoonful of the nourishing broth, he scooped the solid contents into his mouth, savoring the blended items. Setting the spoon down, he glanced at his eldest son seated nearby before a separate small table set with the same dishes of food. His wife was seated at a third longer table together with their younger son and daughter on one side. Across from them sat his daughter-in-law holding an infant beside two young girls, his granddaughters.

He smiled at his granddaughters and urged them to finish their rice. He then cautioned them to keep a watch over their mother who would be busy throughout the day with the new baby, their brother, *his grandson*, he emphasized.

His daughter-in-law who was holding the sleeping infant in her left arm smiled and continued to feed herself with the other hand.

Both granddaughters nodded their heads in obedience, wiggled, and glanced at their Father as they continued to eat using wooden spoons with curved handles.

Next, Farmer Song presented the work agenda. He said that fertilizing the rice terraces below the bend in the trail to the top of the ridge was yet to be accomplished by his second son, Suk Soon, with the help of his Mother. He and his elder son, Suk Chul, would haul the fertilizer up to them before moving over to another area to complete debulking the rocks and terracing the newly dug land on the western side of the same ridge.

Soon after the birth of his grandson, Farmer Song grew increasingly aware of the need to increase the total acreage devoted to rice farming. After all, rice was the most valuable crop for them. Like gold, it could be exchanged for almost anything, even gold itself. Also, it could be stored for years and years, serving as a hedge against bad times, or as insurance against unexpected needs. He anticipated that the title to his land would eventually extend to the eldest son, Suk Chul, and then to the eldest son's firstborn son. The law of primogenitor was the means by which his Father had acquired the land in the first place.

While he himself had no younger brothers, Farmer Song was acutely aware that he had two sons, not one. He expected that his younger son, Suk Soon, would one day also marry and raise a family. His support would depend entirely on the elder brother in exchange for his help on the farm, according to custom.

To assure himself and his sons that there would be plenty for all, he had decided to prepare more land for farming than was actually necessary for them at the present time. That way he rationalized, there would never be any question about the support of Suk Soon and his family, as long as Suk Soon helped with the work. Through the joint efforts of both sons and the largesse of his eldest son, the families along his blood line would live in harmony and mutual support for a few generations to come, he reminded himself.

His wife and their two sons nodded their heads in understanding and agreement to the proposed work plans for the day.

Finally Farmer Song finished his meal and confidently proceeded to proclaim this fact and his satisfaction with the fare with a sonorous, drawn-out burp. He wiped his mouth with the back of his hand and then slowly rose from his seat, using his knee as a fulcrum to hoist himself upright.

His eldest son followed a similar ritual.

The younger son leaned forward towards his nieces and indicated that he might bring each a new surprise from the fields, as he patted each on the head.

He had brought them beautiful shiny rocks and sometimes precious stones spotted while toiling in the fields or crossing the creeks, as well as wild fruits, flowers and even silk worm and butterfly cocoons, they recalled. How their eyes brightened!

The rice Farmer had other parcels of land devoted to growing a variety of vegetables including onion, garlic, several varieties of pepper and cabbage, turnip, carrot, squash, and lettuce. Small clusters of apple, pear, persimmon, quince, grape, apricot, and nut trees dotted his rugged property. It also contained several ponds with lotus plants whose roots and stems were delicious as prepared by his wife. The ponds also supported carp that Suk Soon would catch for eating later in the summer. Wild berry bushes dotted the landscape and wild strawberries carpeted the woods and the slopes.

The climate in this region allowed the Farmer to plant two crops of grain with a good chance of a successful harvest each time. There was enough to provide for his entire family and for bartering at the local village on market days for other goods. He could also provide some rice and vegetables to a distant relative as payment for teaching his younger son to read and write hangul (the phonetic written language) during the long winter months over the past three years.

Outside, Farmer Song surveyed the adjoining barnyard beyond the wall encircling their home. There were other fenced off areas coralling chickens, ducks, a few quail, rabbits, pigs and two cows, a female and the bull, his best friend.

Today, the large beast which had towed the heavy plow unearthing the western slope below the largest pine tree in the field below the ridge would rest, he muttered out loud, as though the beast could hear him. Instead, he expected to harness the cow to help.

The heaviest work was already done to extend his rice acreage by the next season, thanks to the efforts of the bull and his eldest son. The heavy boulders and trees had been removed and the site cut from the western slope of the hill. Now there remained the removal of smaller rocks and large stones in order to remodel the field into a series of terraces designed to permit water to flow from the topmost bank, step-wise, to the bottom field, keeping the rice plants constantly immersed in moisture. He expected the cow would ease the work by pulling the plow to uproot the area and level the terraces over the succeeding days.

First however, Farmer Song and his eldest son, Suk Chul, took up the task of hauling baskets of barnyard sweepings to the rice terraces at the previously designated site. Barnyard manure had been combined with residue from their own pit together with fragments of dried rice stalks, hulls and the kitchen refuse and stored in a large mound near the animal stall. They walked slowly uphill along a narrow trail, each with a wooden frame called a jiggae strapped to his back. A large basket woven from dried rice stalks filled with manure was mounted onto the jiggae and was stabilized with a braided cord. Upon reaching the terrace, the baskets were unhitched and their contents dumped onto the dry ground. Each proceeded downhill for more, moving at a much quicker pace.

After about the tenth trip, a sizeable mound had been amassed despite the fact that the Farmer's wife and younger son, Suk Soon, had dipped into the pile many times already. The fertilizer was transferred with scoops made of dried gourd into smaller baskets strapped around their waists with ties at arms length.

Then his wife and younger son stepped bare-footed into the wet rice fields to scatter the manure by hand. They walked along a line of young rice plants in one direction, crossed over a few rows and reversed directions, all the while tossing the composted manure, moving at a slow, even pace.

Farmer Song's wife had raised her hemline above the knee by hitching her skirt at the waist with a cord. The head cloth shaded her face and her jacket sleeves were rolled above the elbow.

She took up her chanting, now calling on the mountain to yield her flowering beauty for all the world to see, showing off her azaleas (chindalae), hibiscus (moogungwha), and other blossoms. The birds were spreading the news that spring had come already. Now it was time for the flowers to make their showing, she chanted.

Suk Soon listened to his Mother's chanting as he moved in rhythm to her song with his pant legs folded above the knees and his jacket sleeves rolled up. He wore nothing on his head. He had always loved to hear his Mother singing and chanting and could never remember when he was not privileged to hear her. Occasionally, when he was out of hearing range he would whistle softly until he came within range again.

It was nearly noon when Song and his older son headed for the area beyond the craggy hill with the cow in tow to work on debulking the uprooted site of vegetative debris and rocks before smoothing the landscape into terraces.

At least three contiguous stepdown terraces, each one approximately 100 pyeong (one pyeong = 6 square feet) in size should produce enough rice to cover more than an extended family could ever consume, he thought as he worked in the hot sun. Within a season or so, they would sell the extra rice that they harvested and acquire the goods expected for a respectable dowry for his daughter, provide for the tutoring of his grandson, extend the house to accommodate a bride for Suk Soon, and even raise enough for dowries for his granddaughters. All of these things could be done with the extra rice while the current acreage would continue to support his family, even allowing Suk Soon to continue being tutored in the winter months.

He was unable to provide a tutor for his eldest son as he was now able to do for Suk Soon. There were several reasons for this. His first and second born required much care as infants and youngsters, keeping his wife from giving him any assistance in the fields. As an only son, he did not have a younger brother who might have helped with the farming chores in exchange for a share of the yield. He could have looked for an assistant, but that would have required building a separate house for the tenant farmer and his family without the assurrance that the total yield of the farm would support two families.

Once his son and daughter reached a reasonable age, his wife was able to help him with minor tasks. However, by this time other goods were necessary for the young ones which had to be obtained through barter with their produce.

Thus, he was unable to increase his stock of stored grains for other than their own consumption. When his son had grown sufficiently in stature and strength, he began to help the Farmer. In fact, his assistance became increasingly sizeable and significant.

About the time he had reached a reasonable age for tutoring, a series of droughts had also occurred, diminishing yield each year, adding further to the insufficiency of inventory. When his yield had improved to provide an opportunity to send his son off for tutoring in the winter months, his wife became pregnant again.

He had thought her too old to have another child, but she surprised him with the conception and eventful birth of Suk Soon. During her latter period of pregnancy and through Suk Soon's infancy, she was unable to pitch in with the work in the fields. Together, this sequence of events foreclosed any possibility of tutoring for his eldest son, much to his regret. The Farmer had consoled himself knowing that Suk Chul would eventually inherit the land upon his death and therefore would always have the means to provide for his family.

There would be no question about his grandson however, he reasoned. He would be tutored not only in hangul but also in the ideographic writing of China, hanmun. That way, eventually his line would bring scholarship back into the family.

Thus, he continued to toil with his eldest son beside him, with a vision of improving the future of his line by providing more land for cultivation now.

 A WET, SLIPPERY ROCK

At last, the long, long day was coming to an end. He wiped his forehead and face with the sleeve of his shirt, clearing his throat of phlegm which he spat out. He viewed the fields and had a deep sense of satisfaction that what he had undertaken would ensure the brotherhood of the Songs and result in family solidarity and the security of his line for generations to come.

He had heard in his youth that one of his own ancestors who had migrated from China long ago, the middle son of a ruler named Song, acquired sufficient land for himself and his progeny to terminate his dependence on an elder brother. So, his effort to avoid the splitting of families had begun and he was grateful for the insight he had gained to pursue just such a plan.

He noticed that his eldest son Suk Chul had already preceeded him to the house.

He visited the outdoor pit as usual and then sat a while on the veranda beside the portal of the low, stone and mud constructed house. He looked up at the roof, recalling the recent effort he, his sons, and several of his neighbors had put forth to replace the older one. How carefully they had to work to remove the rotten sheaves without damaging the wooden frame of the roof!

Then there was the matter of reconstructing the new covering using tightly bound, dried bundles of rice stalks sloping downward from the central apex. At the lower margins of the roof, the bundles were anchored tightly with bamboo rods placed at right angles to the shafts of the straw, encircling the entire house. It was cool in the summer, dry in the rainy season and it kept the heat from the ondol (floor heating system) from escaping in the winter.

Work had to be done to cover all three rooms at right angles to each other as well as the veranda in front of all three rooms. Goodness! It was a good thing the roof only extended over the cooking area of the small courtyard in front and not the entire veranda, he sighed as he nodded his head and smiled.

The family compound was enclosed by a stone wall surrounding the family's living area separating it from another cordoned area for the livestock. Entry was through a gate set a short distance away. The largest room in the middle served as a living and dining area during the day. At bedtime, the tables were replaced with thin individual pallets for sleeping for the Farmer, his wife and their unmarried children using cloth-covered small blocks for neck support and blankets of different thicknesses for the changing seasons. One of the other rooms was the sleeping area for his son and his family.

The third room was used to store rice and other grains, dried fruits, and drying vegetables and roots. Mulberry leaves were stacked in one corner near baskets of whitish cocoons of silkworms. A wooden loom could be seen in the corner. The room held the harvest and gatherings of the previous season together with all the utensils and stored jars of pickled foods and condiments for the household. It served as part of the kitchen although the actual cooking took place outside, next to the veranda on the hearth. This area was also covered by the roof which slanted and extended to the wall surrounding the compound, but did not extend beyond the verandas of the other rooms.

The hearth was made of a circle of rocks held together by clay. Twigs and wood were added from the top. Towards the veranda, the hearth had an extension all lined with clay reaching under the floor through a conduit with a diameter about the span of a man's hand. This was the kitchen contribution to the ondol system. Heat, odors and gases drawn through this opening traveled through a system of large clay flues that were constructed under the house. In the summertime, the opening was closed. In the winter, heat from cooking was insufficient to warm the house. Fire at this site was maintained throughout the cold with a cover in place to minimize heat loss.

A second site for heating had also been installed located outside the wall that surrounded the main living rooms. This allowed two parallel system of flues for use in heating during the coldest part of winter.

The Farmer pulled off his rubber shoes and began unwinding the strips of linen wound around his legs below the knees to the feet. These strips covered the legs and feet like a stocking and were placed earlier at the start of this long, long day. The cloths were muddy, covered with dirt and debris--evidence of his day-long work in the dry fields and passage through the livestock area and near the rice terraces. He wore them whenever he was not working directly in the wet terraces. Placing them on the wall behind the veranda to dry for the morrow's use, he noticed his eldest son's cloths had already been hung out to dry.

He put on his rubber shoes and walked to the well, placed inside the walled compound, to wash his hands and face and to rinse the dirt off his rubber shoes. And, while he was at the well, he drank deeply from the bucket.

He listened for the little children who could often be heard as they scampered around the house. He did not hear them today. Neither did he hear his wife chanting nor see her familiar form bent over the hearth. This could only mean that dinner preparations had been completed and that the family was awaiting his arrival in the main room.

Turning toward the veranda, he climbed it. He cleared his throat and swallowed the phlegm this time as he stepped bare-footed onto the smooth floor of the main room of the house.

"Yobo (My dear), I could smell your wonderful soup from the outside and I am hungry, indeed!" he called to his wife, who was bent over straightening his seat at the table. Sitting down on a flat pillow on the floor after crossing his legs, frog-like, before the table already set with supper, he smiled at the spread before him.

The menu was similar to breakfast varying only by the vegetables that were pickled and whether or not a piece of meat found its way into the cabbage soup. But it seemed like a totally different meal, coming on the heels of a long and arduous day broken only by sips of water and nibbling on ginseng root.

Picking up the bowl of soup, he drank deeply of the nourishing and fragrant soybean soup, loudly slurping. "Aahh, this is good," he said after which he proceeded to shovel chunks of cabbage and onion into his mouth with his chopsticks. In this manner, with gusto and sheer enjoyment, he completed his meal looking up periodically to see that everyone else was also enjoying the meal.

"Although we have not completed work at the new site, I

shall visit Farmer Park to discuss exchange of polished rice for a basket of unhulked rice for planting and shall return before it gets too dark," he announced at the completion of supper.

He rose from the floor and smiled across the room as his wife also rose from her table to fetch his long-stemmed bamboo pipe laying across the room on another small, low table.

She filled the clay bowl of the pipe with tobacco from a small brass container on the floor, next to the unpainted wooden box filled with dried wide-stemmed straw stalks to use as a light.

Dutifully, after handing the pipe to her husband, she walked to the hearth outside the room with the stalk of straw to light over the dying flames. With mincing steps, she walked back towards her husband, bending slightly forward, cupping her left hand over the lighted stalk held firmly with her right thumb and index finger.

Commenting that he had overeaten again, he puffed on the pipe as his wife tipped the end of the lighted straw into the bowl. After several puffs, he burped loudly as a sign of full enjoyment of the meal, to his wife's modestly concealed delight.

Walking to the edge of the veranda, he stepped into the rubber, boat-shaped shoes his wife bent down to ready for him. He turned towards the main room, smiled, and recounted his blessings to his attentive wife.

He had two sons, the first-born and the last, and now he also had his first grandson! Surely, there would be more grandsons to come. Of course, he also had a daughter between the two sons as well as two beautiful granddaughters.

He continued. His daughter would be ready for marriage in another couple of years. One of the village farmer's sons would certainly be lucky to be selected for his fine-looking and strong daughter, who was such an asset to his family. For did she not know how to tend the garden, care for the animals, tend to the chores aound the house, sew and mend, as well prepare Kimjang and Chusok?

Why of course, not only could she do them well enough to avoid any criticism from the harshest mother-in-law, but she would bear children, too!

His wife agreed with several well-timed bursts of "Kuruum! (Of course!)" whereupon he smiled, and finally signaled goodbye.

Furthermore, he thought as he walked out of the compound, there was his second son, Suk Soon. He was the apple of his wife's heart, a robust and handsome young lad of 14 going on 15, surely the last of his brood of children who was born when he thought his wife had finished such tasks. His birth had brought such pleasure to his wife who even resumed her beautiful singing again, he recounted as he shook his head up and down a few times, in physical agreement with his thoughts.

She had often sung and chanted in the fields as well as at home before they were blessed with any children. However, his wife had stopped singing soon after the birth of their first child, his eldest son. Only the maintenance of quiet would allow that son to sleep. He was fussy and the new mother had difficulty discerning whether his incessant crying was incited by hunger, dyspepsia, or some other terrible discomfort. Only by maintaining silence and tip-toing about the home could she accomplish some of the necessary housework in her harried life. She could no longer assist her husband in the fields and was virtually confined to the house with only brief, furtive trips to the barnyard and pit.

Such restraint extended long after the baby waddled through toddlerhood, extending through their daughter's arrival. The daughter was also fussy, annoying her big brother with her crying. On occasion, both would wail and holler, causing her to clap her hands loudly in an effort to startle them by the distracting sound she made by doing so. This worked more often than not, he had witnessed.

Even after both offspring were well past childhood, she did not sing or chant again, as though a habit of restraint had developed.

Their third child, a second son, appeared more placid than the others, but his wife still did not resume singing. Once in the first few months of life during a crying fit when no amount of rocking or hand clapping soothed or distracted the baby, she instinctively resorted to singing ever so beautifully and gently as a desperate measure to console him. Instantly, the baby quieted down and settled gently upon her breast, not even searching for the nipple, appearing to relax, seemingly content to "listen" to his Mother's singing, she had later told the Farmer. Her chanting seemed to soothe him even more.

Thereafter, her songs and chants returned, bringing comfort and delight to the new baby and to the Farmer's heart, as well. Such songs as Arirang and Toraji could be heard as well as her chanting prayers to Hana-Nim for good weather, good crops, good health, wisdom and happiness as she performed her chores with Suk Soon securely strapped to her back with cloths to support his head against the back of her chest.

How resonating her singing would be to the baby with his ear pinned to her chest, the Farmer had frequently thought to himself.

Farmer Song turned his thoughts to the future. Suk Soon would work for his brother, as expected. In return, Suk Soon and his family would be provided for and, thereafter, the farm would be inherited by the eldest son born to Suk Chul. The reason for the law of primogenitor must be a good one and obeyed.

Suk Soon was a bit spoiled, he admitted, loved to excess by his wife who had begotten him when she thought she had passed her childbearing years. Suk Soon was now learning hangul which might help him in some other way, perhaps leading to a role in the village community.

His second son had a warm personality, breaking out in a winning smile when greeted, reaching out to others with a gesture, a word, another smile. He and Yong Soo, the second son of Lee the Farmer nearest the village, had gotten to become friends through the tutor. Both were being taught at the same time in the winter months. No errand to the village was ever too difficult for Suk Soon, who always volunteered and invariably dropped in for a visit with Yong Soo, according to Farmer Lee. They were similar in age and clearly had become good friends.

All of this was good, he said to himself.

Song puffed on his pipe and approached the part of the creek that edged one tract of his land. It was shallower there and strewn with smooth-topped rocks that could be crossed before the monsoons arrived. Many rocky creeks like this one crossed the farmlands in this mountainous area, cascading step-wise down to the narrow plains below to feed the Naktong tributaries.

This could get him to Farmer Park's house much sooner than walking to the bridge that crossed the creek, up a bit further. He would be forced to use the bridge during the monsoon season, but today the rocks were clearly visible above the water level and he could hurry to and fro with time to play with his grandson before bedtime for everyone.

Puffing on his pipe, he stepped on the first of the several rocks he used to cross the creek each time he went this way. He made his way without difficulty when nearly midway, suddenly, his foot slipped. Stumbling, he fell forward onto the elbow gripping the bowl of his pipe which forced the rigid stem of the pipe to pierce the back of his throat. An immediate searing pain was felt as his mouth welled up with blood. Coughing and sputtering, he gained his foothold and rose from the creek bed. As he pulled the pipe out of his mouth, more blood gushed forth. He spat mouthfuls out and reflexly coughed and gagged as he made his way back toward the bank of the creek.

Wet, bloodied, and dizzy, he turned back and stumbled forward to the house. With every breath, blood leaked into his lungs. He coughed and spat more blood, wiping his mouth with the sleeve of his white jacket, staining it red.

Song's wife had been working with her two helpers, going in and out of the kitchen area singing a ballad when she saw her husband return. She stopped her singing as soon as she noticed his form and the lurching gait. Sensing trouble, she immediately stopped what she was doing and hurried out to him.

Blood was spilling from the corners of his mouth. Together with his drenched, blood-stained clothes, she quickly guessed what had happened.

With panic in her voice, she called for her eldest son, Suk Soon, his sister and her daughter-in-law by name to help her quickly.

"Aiggo, aiggo (Oh my, oh my)!", she shouted as they all hurried forth and helped the injured Farmer over the veranda and into the main room.

She quickly dispatched Suk Soon to fetch the herbalist/medicine man in the nearby village, while she urged Song to stuff his mouth with a kitchen cloth. After washing away the blood from his face and beard, she changed Song's wet clothing with the help of her family. Then she covered him with warm blankets.

Soon, the bleeding had stopped, but only after Farmer Song had lost a lot of blood.

The children were quiet, awed by the events and the tone of dread which filled the air. The baby in the adjoining room had awakened to the sounds and was crying, taking his Mother out from the dizzying activities in the main room.

Suk Soon took the same route as his Father had, reached the creek at the usual safe spot where the smoothened round stones lay. He looked at the rocks, wondered which one was guilty of causing the accident, peered warily at each before stepping forth and sighed with relief as he reached the other side. He scampered up the slope to a dirt road that led several miles to the wall encircling a thatched house where the herbalist and small farmer, Chung, lived.

"Honorable Chung-so bang (Mr. Chung)," he called. "Father has been injured. Please, come quickly and help us!" he pleaded.

A white-haired man with a white goatee appeared at the gate.

Suk Soon immediately proceeded to explain the circumstance surrounding the disastrous event that had occurred at home.

The old man turned back to retrieve a bag and his walking stick before hurrying as best he could to catch up with Suk Soon who led the way.

By the time they arrived, Song was extremely pale and was taking rapid, shallow breaths.

The herbalist/medicine man listened to the wife's explanation of the state in which she had found her husband, examined Song's neck, chest, abdomen, and then peeked into his mouth and throat by moving his tongue out of the way with his fingers. A lesion on the back of the throat, slightly smaller than the diameter of the pipe stem stood out in the center of an area of blood hemmed in by the translucent soft tissues of the back of the throat.

It looked like a puncture wound and would require warm tea treatment and time, he surmised.

He took a particular bag from his sack of herbs and gave instructions for its use as a tea to be drunk several times each day. He wrapped a piece of rabbit hide which he pulled out of the bag and tucked around Song's neck to keep that part of the body warm, for quick healing, he said. Looking serious, he advised quiet and rest and promised he would be back to see if there was improvement and more to do the next day.

All night, the Farmer's wife watched him, adjusting the rabbit hide and the covers, gently stroking his arm whenever he moved. He accepted small sips of the tea made with the herbs up to the late hours of the night. She whispered over and over in prayer, "Hana-Nim, save my husband. Save him, save him!"

By dawn, Song was feverish and drenched with sweat. His breathing was still shallow and rapid. He no longer accepted anything by mouth.

By late afternoon, his skin was cooler and took on a dusky hue with blotches of hemorrhagic spots all over the body. He failed to swallow even the smallest sip of tea and before long became increasingly less responsive. His wife could not determine whether he was still breathing.

By the time the herbalist had returned, Song was totally unresponsive, he was cold to touch and he had evacuated his bladder.

The herbalist turned to Song's wife and said with the saddest voice, "Song-sobang has joined his ancestors, there is no life left."

The wailing began immediately with the wife rubbing Song's

cold, unmoving arm. "What shall I do, we cannot live without you, Song, the Father of my children!" she moaned and wept with tears streaming from her eyes. She was not chanting, she was wailing. She lifted up her skirt and wipped her tears and blew her nose. Turning to her sons flanking her sides, she asked, "What shall we do, my sons, what shall we do? Aiggo, aiggo!".

Both of them were on their knees. They were facing the Farmer who lay cold and stiff, but clean on the mat. They looked down and shook their heads, holding back their tears, unsuccessfully.

His daughter, also kneeling nearby but back a bit, covered her face with both hands and wept unashamedly. Next to her, his daughter-in-law was rocking and consoling the baby in her arms, who had been crying. The daughter-in-law was grimacing at the sudden turn of events. Her two little daughters huddled together closely nearby. Both were wide-eyed and scared.

Seemingly an eternity later, Song's wife wiped her face free of moisture and spoke in a low voice to her eldest son within earshot of Suk Soon. Arrangements had to be made to prepare a grave at the site up on the slope of the hill to the east, where their ancestors were buried. Farmer Park and Yong Soo's family would help, she said. She reminded him to be sure there was sufficient dirt brought from other sites for a proper mound to be made for their Honorable Father.

The local leader of their special religious sect was to be contacted and other relatives and neighbors were to be notified of this tragedy. They would bury their Honorable Father in three days and her son was to kindly request their presence on this occasion, she said.

She asked Suk Soon to help his older brother carry out these duties. The herbalist told her he would also spread the word, as he bowed down to the deceased Farmer's corpse and to his grieving wife, before exiting the house.

Over the next two days, preparations were made for the final presentation and burial of Song, their Honorable Father. Grieving together as a family, each of the sons and the daughter helped their Mother with the multitude of unfamiliar tasks entailed in the preparation of the dead for burial.

Honorable Father was gently disrobed and lovingly washed, all the while carefully covering his pelvic region with a cloth for his wife to cleanse. His skin was dabbed dry and then sprinkled and rubbed with the oily aromatic fragrance expressed from the oval toothy leaves of the hairy plant, the garden balm, that abounded in the woods nearby. It was traditionally used to mask odors and its fragrance was readily retrievable in the oily residue obtained on mashing the leaves with a mallet.

Large blotches of dark hemorrhagic areas could be seen in the skin of the deceased, covering the entire body--testimony to the sepsis that finally ended Father's life.

He was then dressed in the handsome linen outfit he owned and wore only on special occasions. It was white, perfectly in accord with the mourning the family was currently undergoing, perhaps also reflecting what his own spirit experienced at the moment of his mortal demise. The jacket was set neatly over his baggy trousers, while his feet were esconced in white stockings with the pointed ends to rest his toes.

All of this took place with gentle pats and loving touches from members of his family with interruptions to wipe away a drop and even a stream of tears that could not be stemmed in the case of his wife and daughter.

The knot of hair was left for Honorable Mother to fix after drying the strands thoroughly by separating them with fingers drawn through the lengths of the hair shafts. Once dried, his wife wound the greyed hair into a knot on top of his head, holding it in place with the u-shaped pin.

Lastly, his wife combed the Farmer's grey beard with her fingers, giving it a final, ever so gentle tug.

On the day of his burial, the elders of the village of the surrounding farms and their wives gathered at Song's farmhouse where he was laid out on a woven pallet stitched between two bamboo poles, all dressed in the clean white outfit.

After a few words from the religious leader of a sect similar to the Chondokkyo religious group, the bamboo poles of the pallet were lifted by six men, three on each side, who carried the bier to a site on the eastern slope of the property that belonged to Farmer Song. Several circular mounds of dirt now covered with wild grass were located about. A newly dug trough facing east-west lay open and waiting.

The religious leader said a few words again and stepped aside as the Farmer's wife and sons came forward to cover the body with a white cloth, tucking the corners under the head and feet of the deceased. The men who had carried the bïer now lowered it into the ground with the head of the deceased Farmer, facing east. They covered the body with dirt from a pile that had been collected earlier. This continued until they had created a small mound similar in contour and size to others in the area.

Then, the entourage slowly returned to the farmhouse, where several women, who had not joined the burial brigade, had already prepared food for the funeral meal, a vital component to launching off the spirit of the dead from the place of the living.

In addition to the traditional fare for supper, special items were prepared and served. Among these were rice cakes, either soft and filled with a sweet bean paste or doused with a sweet, yellowish bean powder. Rice had also been baked with honey, nuts, and different types of seeds, sesame, perilla and millet, producing a delicious cake. Dried persimmons and fresh fruits were available in a basket. Roasted chestnuts and boiled ginko nuts were offered in small bowls. Bowls of roasted barley tea already sweetened with honey were also readied as a drink. The traditional feast was in honor of the dead and every effort was made to bring forth the best the family could offer.

Everyone ate and spoke in quiet tones, commenting on the special qualities of Farmer Song that each of his sons had inherited. Some of the women even extended the deceased Farmer's qualities to his grandson.

With the people assembled and the movement of the group, the two granddaughters were beginning to recover from their previous retreat. Now they giggled and responded to the greetings of the visitors by hiding behind their Mother's skirt.

Suk Soon sat next to his friend Yong Soo on the veranda before the main room. Neither spoke as they nibbled on the rice cakes and fruits. Before long, Yong Soo bid Suk Soon farewell and indicated that he would see the other at the tutor's house on a regular basis in the coming winter months. With that, Yong Soo joined his parents, an older brother and a younger sister and returned home.

Suk Soon had difficulty falling asleep ever since the night of his Honorable Father's injury. He had grieved each night after his Father's death, dwelling on the loss of his Father, mostly. This evening though, following the burial and the removal of his Father's body from their home, he stared at the darkness and wondered what his Honorable Father might be feeling at the present time. He had not given any thought to death in this manner before and was now confronting it with bewilderment.

He had been told by his parents that Hana-Nim made the world, gave everyone life and took care of everyone.

If this were true, then why did he permit his Honorable Father to die, to be planted under the ground like a seed? What had he done to displease Hana-Nim? How could one know what pleased or displeased Hana-Nim?

Now that his Honorable Father had died and was buried, would he spring up like a plant from a seed?

No, of course not! His body would rot, just like the bodies of animals that he had seen in the woods.

But, what of the spirit of his Honorable Father, would it not rot like the body? He had heard his parents speak of the spirits of their ancestors, but he had never seen them, ever. So, what truth was there that spirits existed? Where were they? In the heavens above, in the woods, in the sea, or up further in the mountains?

Why did some people in the village burn incense before carved figures and pay obeisance to them? Could a man-made structure harbor spirits? Of course not.

He struggled with these questions of mortality, the difference between the spirit of a person and his physical body, and even touched on the idea of immortality. His head felt hot and heavy. He turned sidewards with his hands covering his ears to block out the sounds of the crickets outside, hoping sleep might intervene.

Much, much later--closer to morning, he finally fell exhausted in a disqueting, restless sleep.

UNEXPECTED  CHANGES

After Song's internment and the days of mourning were observed, the eldest son was given the scrolls authenticating his ownership of the farmlands by the signing of the scrolls, which had been kept in a cabinet in the closet of the main room by his parents. The signatures of the leading villagers were needed, the tutor and the major spokesman for the local village. After designating the eldest son Suk Chul as the new owner of the land, each signed his name using Chinese characters and authenticated their signatures by stamping their names beside their personal signatures, using carved wooden blocks and ink. The scrolls were then handed over to Suk Chul in the presence of all members of the family, the two signatories, and the leader of the religious sect to which they belonged.

From the day that Song died, life seemed to have ended for all. From the dawning of each new day, through the various toils of the day, to sunset and the activities of the evening, his absence was deeply felt by everyone.

At the rooster's first call, the widowed wife arose and started the fire to heat water for the rice gruel and tea, reducing amounts of each to amend for Song's absence. They ate in silence, each conspicuously alone, not daring to look at the void left by the absence of the other table and the former head of the household. Even their Mother's singing was no longer heard.

Now, Suk Soon was expected to help with the field chores even more than before. He took up the challenge with great determination, moving the bull out of his stall before harnessing the beast to the plow nearly every morning. He could reach around the creature's neck to drape the harness which he strapped to the plow by either moving the plow forward or the bull backward, depending on the responsiveness of the animal to his tug. Holding the leather strap tautly with both hands, he was even strong enough to lead the animal forward in any direction simply by planting one foot forward and tugging on the strap with all his might. Suk Soon would walk barefooted, not bothering to wrap his legs and feet in cloth, as he cajoled the bull towards the rice fields.

At first his brother would look with relief whenever he saw Suk Soon successfully leading the bull up the hills to the different terraces. But lately, whenever he was within range, his brother Suk Chul shouted, "Hurry up, you're already late! What took you so long? If we don't start right away, the sun will beat up on us! We'll never get to work on the fields that Father insisted on preparing-and maybe, it is just as well!"

Whether this barrage was because Suk Soon was unable to assume the workload Father had borne before, thereby creating a dilemma for his brother, or whether his brother disliked him, was not at all clear to either of them.

As the days, weeks, months, and years passed, hard work had its impact on Suk Soon, who nevertheless continued to grow in height, muscularity, and strength.

The life of a farmer had not been a matter of concern for Suk Soon prior to his Father's death. But now, the reality of the arduosness of this way of life had made its way into his consciousness. Such hard work had its rewards with the bounty of their harvest when Kimjang time came around and there was plenty in the larder. But when times were hard, as when the monsoons were late or in excess or when the locusts came in droves, as happened in succession since his Father's death, what recourse was there for those who tilled the land?

The prayers to Hana-Nim to look favorably on the destiny of the family were not being made by his Mother, who no longer sang or chanted.

However, even in the best of times, his elder brother scolded or spoke harshly to him. He was scolded for not hurrying, for not carrying more of everything, for not digging hard enough, for not planting or gathering the harvest fast enough, for something or other with each of the many tasks that were assigned to him. He was even scolded for being pampered by their Mother!

Suk Soon felt relieved that his brother never worked on the incompleted fields on the western slope. He would not have been able to contribute to the work it would have required. With each scolding, Suk Soon replied, "Yea, yongsa-hasip-sio (Yes, you are right. Please excuse me). I shall try harder the next time."

And he did honestly try harder the next time, but his brother remained dissatisfied. Would there ever be a time when his brother might say, "Sorry, I am pressing you too hard. You are doing alright," wondered the lad?

But there never was.

Two years after his Father's death, his Mother and brother had arranged a marriage for his sister to the eldest son of another farmer in the area. That left Suk Soon and his Mother still occupying the main room. Before long though, his brother and his wife moved into the main room while their Mother slept in the secondary room with her two granddaughters. Suk Soon's pallet was laid out in a corner of the kitchen-storage area at night, where he was expected to sleep. All of these changes were made at the direction of his elder brother, who issued explicit orders for them to be carried out.

Suk Soon had no option but to comply with these changes and he did so with a graciousness that did not escape his Mother's tender heart. But, she said nothing to either son, expecting that someday soon another room would be built to the farmhouse to accommodate Suk Soon and a bride yet to be sought at the right time.

As the patriarch, Suk Chul had denied Suk Soon's continuation with the tutor during the winter months, stating the late rains and locusts had made it impossible to pay the tutor. This edict was understandable, but the long winter days spent in his brother's presence were made all the more unendurable by his irritation with Suk Soon, almost at every step.

To make matters worse, whereas his nieces had enjoyed hearing stories and receiving surprises from Suk Soon while their grandfather was alive, before long, even they shunned his presence in view of their own Father's stern attitude towards him.

Nowadays, it was his nephew who brought joy to Suk Soon. He would scramble to Suk Soon and raise his arms to be lifted. Suk Soon invariably obliged, often following this with a toss and a catch as the child giggled and laughed.

This bonding between Suk Soon and his nephew further aggravated his older brother, who had always been cool to his children, rarely holding any of them in his arms.

At the age of seventeen, Suk Soon was nearly five and a half feet tall. He was strong, handsome, well-tanned and slender, but there was an air of sadness in his appearance which his Mother had noticed for some time. Often she would pat his shoulders and speak soothingly to him.

Whenever his older brother happened to be nearby, he would sneeringly mumble, "What is this? He isn't a baby, even though he acts like one!"

Among the things his Mother would say was that he had to please his brother particularly as he had to consider the possibility of marriage in a few years. His brother's approval was necessary to earn a place for his own family on the farm. Another room could be added to the structure of the house to accommodate his new family until later when a separate structure could be built should Suk Soon's family grow in number. All of these options were possible, but each would require his brother's approval and help, she explained. She mentioned this to him on several occasions, reminding him that this was the custom and his brother would honor his request for support if Suk Soon would carry his load of work on the farm.

On rare occasions when Suk Chul or his wife were not nearby, Suk Soon would tell his Mother of his brother's constant scolding, seemingly never satisfied with his work, no matter how hard he tried.

Hearing this, she would try to console Suk Soon by ascribing Suk Chul's actions to the assumption of the responsibility for the entire family in the absence of their Honorable Father. She said that with time, Suk Chul would reach the level of honor of their deceased Father. Until that time, she urged Suk Soon to do the best he could to comply with his brother's wishes.

She herself would continue to pray silently to Hana-Nim for

harmony between the brothers and among the family members. She would close these conversations by reminding him of the need to consider the future, namely that marriage would require his brother's approval and willingness to provide for Suk Soon's own family.

While he said nothing in reply, he thought to himself, Marriage? What on earth are you thinking of, Mother? I would not marry anyone to live with me under my brother's roof!

One day in late summer, he was sent into the village to deliver farm goods to Yong Soo's family in exchange for a large jug of honey, a specialty of Farmer Lee's wife. Yong Soo happened to be present on their veranda and was clearly eager to talk to Suk Soon.

After the exchange, Yong Soo followed Suk Soon outside the walls of the Lee compound. They sat on rocks along the path to exchange a few words. Yong Soo told his friend of the reading he had done during the last winter's study and how much he had learned about recent events in Korea from the tutor. He told Suk Soon how much he had missed him and asked how he was doing.

Suk Soon told him about their own troubled times with the weather and locusts. Yong Soo's Father had experienced the same, but luckily was able to manage to barter sufficient grain and honey to pay for his continued tutoring.

Among the things he had learned was that other nations besides China, Japan and Russia, for now, were interested in Korea, commercially and strategically. The king of Korea appeared to be powerless and unable to cope with the pressures these countries were placing on Korea, according to the tutor, he said. However, the tutor believed that Korea would soon be open to many nations of the world.

Yong Soo was excited about this and added without hesitation that he would not be bound to the farm, subservient forever to his older brother, but that he would seek life in a town-in a city filled with wonders and culture, where he could learn more about other nations like Japan.

Yong Soo then expounded how his older brother was already taunting him about his expected primacy over their Father's property and how he would have to kow-tow to him, his older brother, in order to have his family provided for. While these words had been said only during the course of a physical battle or two that marred their otherwise fair relationship, the spoken words had lingered long and dug deep into Yong Soo's mind. Yong Soo believed those words were a warning to him from either his departed ancestors, or from Hana-Nim himself to be on the lookout for an opportunity to find another way of livelihood than to be completely dependent on his elder brother.

At this, Suk Soon could not help but open up about his own elder brother and the changes that had occurred since the death of his Father.

Hearing this, Yong Soo looked soulfully into Suk Soon's eyes, trying to discern the depth of Suk Soon's distress. He had noticed a degree of uncertainty in Suk Soon's responses and wondered if he were merely reacting to a recent scolding or whether Suk Soon was sufficiently troubled to entertain a change.

He saw that Suk Soon's eyes were moistened from the tears that he was holding back. Clear enough, thought Yong Soo and he asked his friend to consider leaving Chongsong altogether, joining him in a search for a better life in one of the port cities closest to Japan, Pusan. There they would be able to seek a way of life away from dependence on farming with all of the hard work that it required. There would be opportunities for work in trade between Korea and other countries, particularly Japan. Japan was already trading through the port of Pusan and other countries were knocking at our door, so to speak.

Suk Soon's face lit up. He was excited. In a volley of questions, he asked his friend when he planned to leave, who else was coming, what would be needed, and how they were to survive without the fruits of the farm?

Yong Soo told him the journey to Pusan should be taken by the two of them alone. He suggested they should leave around Chusok (early August) since the weather would still be in their favor. He said he would personally wear all the clothing he owned and would carry food enough for a few days. He had carefully crafted these details from earlier in the spring.

In order not to arouse his brother's anger, Yong Soo suggested that Suk Soon should do the same, wearing extra outfits of clothing and carrying sufficient food for three days.

Agreeing to this, they both looked at each other and vowed a bond of friendship through all climes of life promising to keep these plans a secret for now. They would meet half way between their respective farms sometime about midmorning the same day a week away, each agreed.

Rejuvenated, Suk Soon returned to the farm house with the vessel of honey. He immediately proceeded to the fields to work, but his mind was crowded with emerging details of how to acquire and store enough food for three days that would not spoil without arousing suspicion.

He gathered green fruits, a few nuts and various grains which he stuffed in his pockets and later stored at the bottom of a basket holding all of his worldly possessions.

He wondered how he could effect a smooth departure without arousing reaction, anger or suspicion. It would be easiest to feign a stomach ache and the onset of uncontrollable diarrhea. That way, he could hurry back to the farmhouse, use the pit, and change into the additional clothing. Instead of returning to the fields, he would proceed toward the village. Perhaps if he were lucky, he might even get to have a final glimpse of his Mother.

Coming to grips with the excitement of the prospect of leaving his brother and the sadness of leaving his beloved Mother left him unreactive to the usual scathing comments delivered by his brother during the remaining days.

TOWARD TONG-HAE, THE EASTERN SEA

The midmorning sun was extremely bright. Suk Soon was sweating under the three jackets and three trousers he had put on. Already the small basket with the fruits, nuts, and grain seemed heavier than it really was.

He had gotten a glimpse of his Mother, who was busy washing clothes by the well. She had looked up for a moment and smiled, but continued to beat the wet clothes laid out on a flat stone with washing rods clutched in each of her hands. Drawing water from the well, she rinsed the pieces before repeating the rhythmic beating once again. He wished he could hear her singing, but was even grateful to hear the rhythmic beat, beat, beat of the sticks.

Out he proceeded, hurrying down the path as if to catch up with his commitment to work. Instead of taking the turn towards the fields however, he took the opposite turn, the one that led towards the village.

It was not long before he saw a familiar figure approaching. It was Yong Soo, who was also sweltering in the midmorning sun, looking strangely plump under the additional clothing that he wore. Instead of a basket, he had a cloth bag slung over his shoulder, presumably with food enough for several days.

The two young men shouted at each other, calling out the other's name. Once they were abreast, they hugged each other and then sat down for a moment of relief. They removed their extra clothing, placing them in Yong Soo's bag while the food was transferred to Suk Soon's basket. Each took an apricot out of the basket, sucked on the fruit pulp, and perfunctorily spat out the seed. Refreshed, they rose and crossed the adjoining field together, headed south, southeast.

They walked on and on across fields, through woods, down craggy hills and stopped near rapidly moving streams, where they refreshed themselves with long drafts of cool water. Before long it began to grow dusky.

Settling near a small stream, they nibbled on wild berries gathered along the the way together with some of the grain from their bags, washing mouthfuls down with water scouped by hand from the nearby stream.

By dark, magpies amongst the trees squawked loudly overhead as the young men prepared to settle down for the evening. The intermittent croaking of the frogs and the buzzing of the cicadae created a musical background interrupted only by the noisy magpie sounds.

Together with their fatigue from the long day of travel and the coolness of the evening, an early slumber came to each of them, as they curled up on the slope next to the trickling stream.

The light of the early sun and the chirping of a variety of birds in the absence of the squawking, croaking, and buzzing awakened them. Glad to be in each other's company, they looked at each other, smiled, then stretched, yawned, and declared, "At last, we are free from the tyranny of bossy older brothers!"

Before long each was looking in the basket for something to eat. Grain, nuts, and fruit together with the cool water made a wonderful breakfast. During their meal, they agreed to make great progress that day, all the while looking for additional edible items on their journey to the shores of Tong-hae and eventually, Pusan.

In this manner, they traveled more than a week headed south, southeast. Once it rained, forcing them to slow down and seek refuge under a craggy outcropping of granite, the major rock forming the peninsula of Korea. When the rain stopped, they continued on their way, and while it seemed interminable, neither was discouraged. And, each felt the target of their destination would appear before long. Neither had any idea how long it would take to reach Tong-hae or Pusan by foot, through a very mountainous and rugged country.

There were many, many interesting sights that had diverted their sojourn, but only briefly. They saw burial mounds that were so large, they seemed like real hills. Surely, the interred must have been of royal blood, they thought. Beautiful buildings dotted the area, too. Some were hidden away in the woods, all painted ornately with designs, predominantly with green, black and red. Many housed statues of a seated Buddha with his eyes closed and his hands in various effeminate postures. Ornate stone stupas stood before some, evidently the work of true artisans, they conjectured.

As they progressed, they ran into villages that seemed larger and much more crowded than their own village of Chongsong. They stopped here and there to work as extra hands in the fields for a day or two after bargaining with farmers for fruits and grain.

During these brief work arrangements, they were even treated to rice, soybean soup and pickles. They had come to crave this simple meal and the rich aroma emanating from the cooking over open fires reminded them of their own homes and the Mothers they had left behind. Undaunted though, they continued to head south, southeast.

Finally, three weeks after their departure, they saw a bluish-gray outline on the horizon to the east. It was Tong-Hae or the Eastern Sea, Yong Soo claimed. Neither had ever seen the sea before. They were mesmerized by it's vastness, as it covered the entire eastern horizon. Greatly encouraged, they resumed their walking with increased vigor, now heading directly eastward.

Hills and short valleys blocked out the view of the sea from time to time, but the sea continued to reappear once these obstacles were cleared.

Eventually, they reached the beaches north of Pohang. Many little farms dotted the inland landscape a short distance away from the sandy shores. The shoreline itself was craggy and short, lined with rocky ground that appeared to fall into the sea. Fingers of rocks appeared out in the water as the waves washed back and forth onto the shore.

At the shore, they noticed the ground was different-it was covered with sand and pebbles. Unlike the rather uniform firmness of dirt, sand was unpacked and coarse in texture, tan in color but peppered with small smoothened rocks of darker color of variable sizes. There were living and dead sea creatures about on the shore and seaweed washed back and forth with the tide. The air smelled salty and organic and the swish, swoosh of the sea was constant. White sea gulls and herons flapped about with the gulls squawking loudly now and then.

Both of the young men took off their rubber shoes, rolled up their trousers and walked into the water with expectant joy. The sand felt different than anything they had ever walked on before. It was firm, not squishy like wet soil; it was smooth and fine, unlike the rocks they encountered on the farms or along the creeks that peppered the landscape in the region of Chongsong. Walking further and further into the sea with exuberance, their long braids soon became soaked with the briny water.

Suddenly, a large wave appeared and rushed at them, driving them back towards the shore. Each was surprised by the size of the wave and their fearful reaction to it. Laughing at the scare they shared, they returned to their belongings already set up on higher ground.

Several people were nearby: men with straw hats tied under their chins and women with hoods like their mothers wore. Some of the women were carrying baskets of sea weed on their heads, stabilizing the baskets with one hand. A few men were carrying baskets of fishes of various sizes and species from small wooden boats docked nearby next to a wooden pier. Most of the people were headed to small buildings set further up on the shore. Yong Soo and Suk Soon meandered towards the first of the buildings to explore.

In these buildings people were sorting out the catch, hanging flat pieces of sea weed or laver on wooden racks and resorting shells and other sea foods into brass containers of seawater. Still, others appeared to be exchanging funny-looking coins with holes in them for various items.

There was a din and special odor in these areas, something neither of the boys had ever heard nor smelled before. The sound was due to the collective calls of the sellers to the shoppers of the nature and cost of their ware. Each extolled the freshness and quality of the sea fare, while promising a fair exchange.

The concentrated odor of fresh sea food did nothing to their appetites, but it did not take them long before their appetites were whetted. Near the other end of the building, they encountered men and women who were broiling fish on a brass stove. One man was loudly calling the attention of the shoppers to the freshness of his ware. The delicious aroma aroused their appetites, as they stood by watching the man lift his lightly charred specimen onto a brass platter with a wooden spatula.

Realizing they had nothing with which to exchange for the fish except their bundled pieces of clothing in the bag, Yong Soo impulsively pulled one of his own linen jackets out. Waving the jacket, Yong Soo asked the man how many broiled fishes he would exchange for it.

The man looked Yong Soo over, then eyed the jacket closely and fingered the texture of the fabric. Then announcing rather loudly that he was going to be magnanimous, he said that he might exchange four broiled fishes for the very "small" jacket, emphasizing the size of the piece. He reminded them that the fishes were freshly caught, while the jacket had been used. However, he was willing to make the exchange since the jacket just might fit one of his sons.

Such a bargain was too good to pass for the two hungry boys. So it was that the boys from a farming community in the mountains of central Korea had their first taste of char-broiled freshly caught sea bass, hot off the grill! Each devoured two whole good-sized fishes, sucking the eyeballs and spitting out the lenses with gusto at the end.

Licking the savory skin and remnants of the fish off their fingers, they made their way towards the shoreline to wash their soiled appendages. They shook off the excess water off their hands and then retreated above the water line.

The young men sat down and stretched backward on the sand, closing their eyes. Each wore a wide smile on his face. They had arrived at the shores of Tong-Hae. They had tasted of her bounty. And, each was grateful to Hana-Nim for bringing him to this point on a journey to find a better way of life than to live under a brother's intolerable dominance.

Before long, the heat and brilliance of the sun raised them from their brief rest. They agreed to remain in the area for a few days. By seeking work, they could even collect sufficient coins for use on their way to Pusan. The sea was inviting and they hoped to be working on a fishing boat, even though neither had ever been in a boat before, nor knew how to swim.

They wandered about conversing with the fishermen, inquiring about any need for paid assistance. One of them, Kim by surname, said that he could use both of them, one on-board the boat to seek, bait, and haul in the catch and the other on-shore to work with the nets and the catch. They would be fed and given a fraction of their harvest each day in exchange for these services, he indicated. Once a week fishing was repeated at dusk using lighted lamps hanging over the boat to attract the squid. And, this was the day for squid fishing, he told them.

The boys quickly accepted the offer. Yong Soo elected to work on the boat and Suk Soon did not protest, innately preferring to work on solid ground rather than at sea. While the Fisherman and Lee were asea, Song would help to untangle piles of nets in the corner and repair damaged nets, as shown by the Fisherman's wife. After the boat returned, handling and processing of the catch would be done by all of them before the day's task was done, they were told.

After this brief on-shore orientation and demonstration, they were treated to a hearty supper just inside the Fisherman's shed.

After supper, the Fisherman and Yong Soo stepped into the lighted boat and headed just off shore to hunt squid.

It was way late in the evening when the boat returned. Fisherman Kim and Yong Soo were elated with the size of their catch. Suk Soon had never seen live squid before and quickly discovered that its tentacles could latch onto your hand, unmoved by repeated shaking of the hand to which it clung, requiring the use of the other hand to pull at the squid to relinquish its hold.

After the hustle and bustle of hauling the bounty and nets off the boat into the shed, they worked by the light of oil lamps hung on poles dotting the area. Much time was spent untangling the squid from the nets, a formidable task as the creatures seemed to cling to the nets even after dying. Before long they had a large cartilaginous pile of squid to be sold prior to, or after drying in the sun, over the coming days.

Anchovies had also been caught closer to shore on their return to the pier. Apparently, evening and the lights from the boat attracted them also. The smaller nets used for the anchovies also had to be picked off these variously sized creatures. Smaller fishes were placed in shallow broad baskets to be left to dry over the coming days. Larger ones were cleaned before placement together with rock salt into dark clay pots.

The mixture was then ground by mashing with a wooden bat until the texture was that of a rough gruel. These were to be used to flavor various pickles and dishes after slight fermentation had occurred to enhance their flavoring power. The vessels were covered with cloth and tied with a cord before they were stacked in a corner to reach the proper degree of ripening.

By dawn their work was done and after drinking bowls of a fermented rice drink called makale, which the Fisherman brought out from the back of the shed, all three were overcome by light-headedness and a peculiarly happy mood. Before long, each stretched out on the floor in the shed and fell soundly asleep on piles of dried netting.

At the sound of the creaking of a wheelbarrow, Suk Soon awakened to find the Fisherman's wife carting piles of squid and several of the stacked baskets of small anchovies out of the shed to dry in the outdoor sun. She was used to the Fisherman's work habit of sleeping in the shed after a long night's work instead of returning home up towards the hill on days after squid fishing. These took place once a week and she always came down from the farm early in the morning to complete the further processing of the bounty for the market.

She had already prepared rice, pickled vegetables and sea food for her husband and his workers and had set them on a small table near where her husband lay. She called to her husband who was rousing, invited Suk Soon and Yong Soo to join him, and wished each a hearty meal.

Yong Soo smelled the food even before he opened his eyes. He sat up, bowed to the Fisherman's wife and quickly joined the others at the table. All three lost no time in slurping up their food with gusto.

That day and the next, they cast off early in the day, bringing back their catch before dark. There was a great variety of sea life in their hold including large crabs, lobsters, small tortoises, sea bass, breem, snapper, grouper, variously sized tuna, small sharks and seaweed of various kinds. The Fisherman called out the names of the various creatures as he tossed them into buckets of sea water to keep the live catch fresh.

Suk Soon quickly learned to tell them apart and also how to grasp and toss each species without injuring himself. He also hauled the life-giving ocean water by the dock back to the shed using two buckets at a time to extend the freshness of the live ones for market.

They stayed for a couple of weeks, exchanging the stock of dried and fresh fare which they received as payment for coins. After they had each amassed a handful of coins, it was time to head on down towards Pusan.

They told the Fisherman of their decision and were surprised by his look of sadness and dismay. The boys had helped to increase the yield and both the Fisherman and his wife had come to enjoy the increase in their coin collection, let alone the pleasure of their company. The Fisherman tried to talk them into staying longer, but was not successful. So, he finally accepted their wish to move on and bid them well and good wishes.

The Fisherman advised them to avoid the shore at a point where it headed north because of a land extension. He told them the shoreline would turn south again like the curve of a rabbit's tail many miles later. Crossing over land at Yakjon to Taejin would save them miles of walking. This part of Korea was like the tail of a rabbit, he had laughingly told them. They should then reach Gampo village before heading further south to Pusan. The Fisherman did not know the land or seascape below Gampo and was unable to give them an estimate of how much longer their journey might take to Pusan.

The young men proceeded along, avoiding the tail of the rabbit, crossing over to Taejin instead, as advised. They reached another cluster of fishing buildings again with farmlands set quite a ways back inland. From the shore line looking out into the sea, they saw an arm of land stretching out against the horizon, hugging the huge bay spread before them. This was Gampo. The bay was busy with fishing boats of all sizes and the shore was crowded with buildings like those in the village they had recently left.

They lingered here for a couple of days. This time, they did not have to work but used a few of their coins, instead. They saw the advantage of the coin as a device to effect a trade when one did not have an item of equal parity to trade for what one wanted. With coins or money, trade could center about a single item, allowing greater freedom to the buyer who gave up the coin and the trader who could purchase whatever with the money obtained from the trade.

Continuing their journey walking southward along the shore after a seemingly interminable span, they saw a rock formation cropping out in the distant sea. The closer they got to the shore before it, the more intrigued they became. The formation was also inviting, tempting them to clamber onto it to cool down, perhaps even to search the rocks for edible snails and mollusks.

After agreement to this option, Yong Soo dropped his bag on the sand and dashed forward. Suk Soon followed suit. It did not take long before they realized that the rocks could not be reached by walking without becoming completely immersed in the sea. Since neither could swim, they wetted themselves up to the neck before they turned back to shore with their braids dripping with water.

The rocks formed the tomb of an ancient king named Munmu who wanted to be buried in the East Sea so that his spirit could guard the East Sea forever, they learned from others nearby. Looking solemnly at the rocks and the sea around it, they could almost feel King Munmu's spirit surging in the surf, now reaching the shoreline, then pulling back to make sure the shore was clean and smooth, over and over again. After staring at the formation for some time, they quietly agreed to linger just that one day before proceeding towards Pusan in the morning.

It took a few more weeks before they reached Pusan because of their penchant to visit everything new along the way.

Pusan was like no other village they had ever seen. In fact, Pusan was not a village, but a city. There were many large buildings with tile roofs and the streets were lined with stones. The streets were lit with lamps of oil hung on tall wooden poles. Horse drawn wagons carried people, not only goods. There were even covered carriages drawn by horses directed by a single driver perched forward without a cover. Clearly, these belonged to people of high status. There seemed to be many of such status, they agreed, as the streets were bustling with people all dressed up. It seemed like what they had imagined the capital of Korea, Seoul, to be. After wandering around the city a bit, they retreated to the coast, sticking to the fisheries and boats.

There, they found another fisherman, Chun by name, who seemed impressed with accounts of their work experiences. They were offered the right to use a corner of the shed as their living quarters, two meals a day (breakfast and supper) and a small wage for their services. The offer of a place to sleep with two meals a day in addition to money seemed too good to be true to both of them. They promptly agreed.

Yong Soo worked on the boat as before, laying out the nets and bait, hauling the catch and looking out for rocks. Suk Soon stayed on shore, working with the nets, repairing them and untangling them while awaiting the return of the boat. Once the boat was in, all three of the men worked with the haul as they had done in the other fishing villages. The weather had been cooler affecting the species that were caught, compared to earlier ventures.

Each looked forward to the end of the week when they had a

free day. On their free day, they put on a clean set of clothes and moved towards the inner city to explore and enjoy themselves.

People crowded the streets and stalls before the market to which they were headed. Hawking salesmen and women manned the stands where goods of every imaginable sort were being sold for money. Food stalls were also plentiful, tending to be grouped together. Raw, packaged goods and cooked foods were being bought by women mostly, but some men were also carrying baskets. These baskets got progressively filled as the patrons made their way from one end of the market area to the next.

At the end of the market area, there were a couple of newer, small buildings before which stood several men eyeing the market area. All five of the men looked foreign. Each was a bit shorter than the average Korean with somewhat darker eyes and more facial hair about the face. Most outstandingly, however, none had a top knot or braids. In fact, their hair was shorn off leaving only about an inch of tuft sitting straight up. Two wore a cap with a visor and the rest were bare-headed.

These men were Japanese who were workers for a shipper of goods to and from Japan. They were watching the movement of their goods being sold in the market. Their ships had imported tea, gingko nuts, bamboo products and one shipload had brought a variety of Japanese woven cloth as well as brass and lacquered wooden objects. Most of these items were novel, attracting much attention from the shoppers, who were curious and sometimes willing to purchase various ones for a set number of coins.

Yong Soo and Suk Soon wandered toward the men, greeted them and proceeded with small chatter.

The men were quickly disarmed by the smiles and warmth of

the greetings. They were recent arrivals from Japan and had only acquired bare rudiments of Korean. By resorting to the use of gestures and simple words to establish baselines for communication however, it did not take long before it was understood that both groups were new to Pusan.

Inspite of their language differences, they understood about their common wish to sample the local makale-a drink of renown even to the Japanese. They did not have to do much searching. Signs were posted over quite a few shops and stalls in hangul and Japanese, declaring they served the best makale in Pusan. All agreed on the one which seemed large enough to accommodate their number.

Kato, Sakai, Nishimura, Yamamoto, and Tanaka were pleased with their new acquaintances. They referred to Yong Soo and Suk Soon as Lee-san and Song-san. Together they laughed and continued to communicate using words embellished with gestures. Before long, Lee-san and Song-san were able to speak a few words of Japanese.

The Japanese were longshoremen, unloading and loading ships that traveled from Japan to Pusan and back to Japan. They loaded the ships with large amounts of timber collected from the central regions of Korea as well as coal and iron ore transported from the northern regions of Korea by horse-drawn wagons.

Loading was worse than unloading, they said. In fact, they were very shorthanded. Their bosses had not yet succeed in recruiting sufficient numbers of Japanese to work in Pusan. They were to rotate back to Japan after a few months and had been doing this for only the past few weeks, they said. They already missed their homeland and were very glad that Lee and Song were friendly, they continued.

Then they casually raised the question of the interest of Lee-san and Song-san in their line of work. They were certain that work for a salary was possible for them.

Laughing and agreeing with each other by frequent nodding of their heads, they spent several hours together in fellowship refreshed by the makale. Much later, they parted urging Lee-san and Song-san to consider working with them and they promised to meet again the following week.

A BRIEF HISTORICAL BACKDROP

This and other encounters between these two young men from the central mountainous farm regions of Korea and the temporary workers from Japan were set during a period of monumental political developments in the region.

Japan had long-standing interests in Korea, which brought her into conflict with other countries, namely China and Russia, with similar regard for the peninsula jutting off the southeastern end of the continent of Asia. Battles and treaties had been used to wrestle with each other for dominance over Korea. Progressive elements in Korea revolted against the King of Korea on two occasions early in the 1880's supported by the Japanese. China sent help with troops forcing the Japanese to retreat. This was followed by a treaty between China and Japan, the treaty of Shimonoseki in 1895. Both China and Japan would officially recognize Korea's independence and autonomy. However, Japan did not honor the guarantee of independence for Korea, making demands and forcing the King to flee to the Russian legation.

Tensions and war followed between Russia and Japan over the Korean issue. In 1904, Japanese troops entered Korea as a springboard for military operations against Russia. Supposedly, Korea would be independent with Japan serving an advisory position. Eventually a treaty was signed between Japan and Russia in 1905 where it was agreed that Japan held the paramount position of influence and interest on Korea. The western powers, namely England and the United States, agreed to the treaty.

Upon this political background, the Japanese seized the opportunity to tap into the abundant raw materials from the northern regions of Korea in the early 1900's. After all, Japan was a volcanic collection of islands with insufficient natural resources, totally dependent on her neighbors for the raw materials which she converted into goods for trading worldwide to support her growing economy and international posture.

Japan began to send military and commercial elements to effect a gradual takeover of Korea and it was only five years later that Japan formally annexed Korea.

This history and more current developments were not known to the vast majority of Korean peasants. Neither Lee nor Song was fully aware of the developments that led to the current status of affairs between Korea and Japan. In fact, everything seemed quite fair to them, particularly as these men were friendly and no tension was evident at all.

ROCKS IN TONG-HAE

That unforgettable morning, Lee and Song awoke and noticed that the sky was dark and overcast. At breakfast, Fisherman Chun commented to them that fishing was usually better under such a cloud cover and they should expect a bountiful harvest for the day.

The boat was readied and the fisherman hauled in the anchor. Lee was already working with the bait as the boat pulled away from the pier.

Song swung his arm in an arc to wave, quite glad to be the shoreman on a day like this. The water was choppy with an occasional swell spilling over the pier, wetting everything in the way. Considering this was at the end of the bay, Song surmised that it would be very rough out on the sea in such a relatively small boat. He returned to the shed and began to untangle and repair the damaged nets from the previous long day's work.

Near the end of the day, long past the time when the boat would have returned, Song grew increasingly anxious, frequently pausing to look out to sea, looking for the return of the familiar boat.

All day the wind had whooshed about, lifting the rafters of the shed, knocking down racks and overturning barrels and poles. Thunder had rumbled off and on, preceeded by bolts of lightning that lit up the bay.

Song was now joined by Mrs. Chun. Both peered out hoping to see the familiar flags on the center mast of Chun's boat on a returning one. Several boats could be seen slowly weaving their way towards land, rocking unsteadily as they reached the pier, but none was Chun's.

Mrs. Chun ran out to meet the crew of each one, asking of the gravity of the storm at sea and whether Chun's boat might have been spotted.

The answer was the same each time-yes, the storm was very, very bad. No, they had not seen Chun's boat, but it should return soon, everyone assured her.

Much later in the evening after the storm had quieted down considerably, Mrs. Chun and Song heard another boat docking at the pier. They rushed out with anticipation, but were quickly disappointed again when they saw that the boat was not Chun's.

The three fishermen on the boat called to Mrs. Chun almost in unison, "Aiggo, Chun-sobang manora (Oh dear, Mr. Chun's wife)!"

She stopped in her tracks with a chill running down her back.

One of them continued, "We have very bad news for you. Your husband's boat rammed into a pile of rocks out at sea which everyone always skirts around. The storm raised the water and masked the rocks. We saw his boat strike the rocks, break apart and sink immediately. He and all aboard perished, because we found no survivors when we finally reached and searched the site."

"We were only able to salvage this hat which was floating in the area. We knew it to be your honorable husband's."

The three chimed in together, "We are so very, very sorry to bear such bad news."

Mrs. Chun quickly took the hat and examined it. It was her husband's hat, indeed. Filled with fear, in desperation she shouted, "Aiggo, aiggo. What has become of my husband? Why did you not see him?"

"Perhaps he is still in the water, clinging on to a piece of the boat, waiting for someone to pull him out! Please, please go back and look for him! Won't you, please?" she pleaded.

The fishermen shook their heads and said that there was no sign of life around the debris, assurring her that they had searched and searched the area thoroughly for some time, even endangering themselves, to no avail.

By now, others around the fishing pier had heard the terrible news and began to gather to console Mrs. Chun. Everyone dreaded such an occurrence--awaiting the return of their loved ones with bated breath whenever a storm raged, well aware of the risk to fishermen each time they went out to sea.

Song was devastated! His best friend, no, his only friend, Yong Soo Lee, had also perished in the storm along with Fisherman Chun. He sought comfort from those around him, but found they were absorbed with Mrs. Chun and her grief more than the loss of his friend whom they barely knew.

He slowly turned to walk towards the beach. The wind and the sand whipped across his body, but he continued his way to the shoreline, undaunted, as though in response to a call from the spirit of his friend. Wetting his feet in the sea water, he looked up at the dark sky, wondering again about what happens to the spirit of a man after death. He imagined Yong Soo meeting his Honorable Father somewhere in the spirit world, telling him of their adventures and their hopes for bettering their lives.

He thought of Fisherman Chun, a kind and generous man who brightened their lives. He imagined him casting his net out among the clouds in the sky. Would he catch a star, perhaps?

Getting drenched, he quickly backed off towards the shore. Deeply saddened and now getting angry, he shook his fist at the sea and vowed it would not get him. He bit his lower lip and said outloud with great pain, "The only companion I have had since my escape from tyranny, my best friend is dead! I am alone, and I do not know what to do!"

He grieved the rest of the night, alternately walking along the shore when the rain let off or pacing the floor under the cover of the shed when it poured. Soon the light of dawn lightened the sky, announcing the arrival of yet another day. There was little that Suk Soon could do except to take his and Yong Soo's effects and move on, he decided.

Among Yong Soo's things he discovered a tiny book with thin pages. It was a dictionary of Chinese characters (hanmun) with the equivalent in hangul. He did not know how to read the Chinese characters, but decided to hang on to the book for now. Perhaps, he would one day be able to use the book. Certainly, it would always be a reminder of his companion and his hope to use it to better his life.

Over the next several days, after helping the grieving Mrs. Chun to prepare the shed and its contents for sale, he bid her farewell, bowing low in respect for her and in deep sorrow for her loss.

He stuffed Yong Soo's bag with his personal things, including the book, and hurried off to the market in search of other work and another place to stay. He had made up his mind that he would not tempt the sea with his life for the foreseeable future.

He walked away from the piers, towards town. It was near noon. He had seen buildings with crosses on the roof and had wandered about them. The one before the market area was small and several people stood about engaged in conversation.

As he attempted to cross the street on his way to the market carrying the bag that Yong Soo had brought from Chongsong, one of them asked if he needed help with a place to stay. Bewildered, Suk Soon noticed their smiles and could feel their warmth as one of the older men reached out for his bag, setting it down on the ground before him. They asked him again, following this up with other questions.

It did not take long for Suk Soon to admit that he did, indeed, need a place to stay.

They invited him into the Church, leading him towards the back. The inside was unfurnished, but for a lectern close to the back wall. Through a door at the back wall, they entered another room where several men sat on a clean floor before small tables eating their noonday meal of rice, soup and a few other dishes.

Suk Soon was invited to join them and one of them quickly made space for him to sit, another produced bowls and utensils from a basket in the closet, and still another served him some of the same fare from pots set on a low table standing in a corner.

Suk Soon was overwhelmed with their kindness and consideration. He was ready to join in the feast when the people who had brought him in kneeled down, folded their hands in prayer and recited in unison, "God is great, God is good and we thank Him for our food. Amen."

"Now, you may eat," they said with great kindness.

Suk Soon learned that the group was Christian, linked to the Presbyterian Church of the United States of America (USA). Missionaries had established the local church and they were helping people in many areas.

He was invited to stay as long as he needed to with no obligations other than to clean his area and to attend the services at the Church on Sundays.

They explained that the same Hana-Nim tried to reach humans through prophets, but was unsuccessful in convincing stubborn, sinful Man. Thus, he sent his only Son in the form of a baby who was born to a Virgin in Bethlehem nearly 2000 years ago. That Son, called Jesus, grew to be a man. At the age of 30, he preached, interpreting the Words of God for all to obey. He was hated by unbelievers who nailed him to a cross. After his death, he was entombed in a cave, but arose on the third day. He eventually ascended to Heaven to be with God and promised that if we obeyed God's commandments, and there are ten of them, we would also ascend into Heaven to be with God or Hana-Nim after our own deaths.

Because he already believed in a supreme God, Hana-Nim, he did not find their concepts difficult to understand or accept. As a matter of fact, their beliefs seemed to extend from his and his family's belief in a supreme, though somewhat distant God. Suk Soon found it easy to incorporate them into his own deeply imbedded belief in an all powerful God.

Before a week had gone by, he learned from the men and the people connected with the Church that workers were being recruited to work on sugar cane plantations in Hawaii, an island in Tae-pyung-yang (the Pacific Ocean). The Church had representatives in Hawaii to ensure their proper treatment and the retention of their customs in the new environment. Salaries were said to be good and lots of Koreans were signing up.

Suk Soon did not consider such a move to be just right at the present time, he said. He needed to look at all options in Pusan, first.

When the day and about the time he and Yong Soo had agreed to meet their Japanese friends had come around again, he headed off alone to meet them.

He had not expect to find the group of Japanese workers in the market itself, but he bumped into them mingling with the shoppers. After the excitement of their mutual recognition was over, they asked about Lee-san.

Song told them about the tragedy using his hands in reference to the boat, the storm, the sea, and the rocks. He tried hard to maintain a straight face, but his eyes sparkled with wetness.

They shook their heads and looked down at their feet, sucking air through one corner or the other of their lips, in sympathetic understanding of what had transpired. Their genuine sorrow on hearing the news was more than Song had expected from comrades with whom they had only spent one drinking spree together.

The Japanese grabbed ahold of Song's arm and led him outside the busy market. They motioned and asked him if he wanted to join them as a longshoreman. Their boss had consented to consider both Lee-san and Song-san as coworkers with them. They would take him to the boss the following morning, but for now he could join them. In fact, they had living space for him in their quarters and he was welcome to join them immediately, they said.

Unbelievably, Hana-Nim is looking out on my behalf, thought Song. Yes, he would join them and see the boss in the morning. He expressed his genuine gratefulness to them for allowing him to stay with them, promising to reimburse them for cost of his share of living together and then left them briefly to retrieve his effects from the Church.

And so, Song joined these men, working as a longshoreman unloading and loading ships owned by the Japanese. It did not take long to find out that work was more arduous loading than unloading the goods.

Timber had to be handled by teams of 4-6 men, depending on the length and diameter of the wood. First, they had to be removed from wagons drawn by teams of horses and piled near the pier for later transfer onto the ship's hold. The subsequent maneuvering of the large heavy, rigid cargo into the hold of a ship was especially difficult. A designee had to call out the strategy to align the timber appropriately as the men choreographed their steps, turning a bit here, reversing more there, and so forth. Each piece had to be placed so as to minimize imbalance of the ship, taking care to prevent each from rolling during the journey, especially in a wild storm.

Piles of coal and ore were also transported to Japan in these ships. These had to be shoveled from carts to the pier prior to hauling the cargo by basketfuls into the ship's hold.

Climbing up the plank and down the steps made it necessary for Song to quickly purchase shoes that tied over the instep by cords. The traditional rubber boat-shaped shoes he had used would slip off, once nearly causing him to tumble down into the hold during one of these treks weighted down with a large, heavy basket of ore.

After a full day's work, the men were tired, ready for food, makale, and rest. Song-san had been provided with space enough to stretch for sleep. He bought a pallet, blankets and a few other essentials at the market with money he had earned earlier from Fisherman Chun.

The men ate rice which they boiled along with a broth made with soybean sauce called miso. This was topped with chopped scallions and tofu purchased on the way from work. Several crocks lining the corner of the kitchen area contained pickled items including a cherry called ume, turnips, small olive-sized whole onions, and ginger slices. The soup and rice were ladeled out to each in small lacquered wooden bowls and a central pile of pickles was available for selection by picking amongst these choices with their individual lacquered wooden chopsticks. Someone always remembered to purchase a slab of raw fish on his way from work each day. The fish was shared after being cut into pieces and was served over freshly shredded turnips to be eaten with soy sauce.

The soup was much lighter in flavor and content than the soybean soup Song was used to, but he quickly got used to the new flavor. The pickles preferred by his new comrades were sweetened, not hot like Korean pickled goods. But again, he quickly got used to theirs.

Song contributed a portion of his salary to a common pool and helped with the cleaning and straightenening of their living space. His larger stature, impressive strength and general helpfulness with each of their tasks at work and at home together with his warmth and friendliness made for their quick bonding. There was harmony and a sense of comraderie shared by the men as a group.

Song quickly learned their language, speaking quite well, although he never could quite abolish a decided Korean accent. He also taught them to communicate with Koreans for which they were grateful. Thus, in real harmony, their friendship grew.

Months later, the Japanese were ready to rotate back to Japan. Song became a bit apprehensive about meeting an equal number of others who were slated to take their places. Because of his seniority at the workplace in Pusan, he was expected to lead the newly recruited Japanese men through the paces of the job.

As it turned out, this experience as the head honcho helped to return some of the confidence he had lost under his elder brother's hard press. Song liked working with the new Japanese workers and they seemed to like him in return. Living arrangements were pretty much the same and they continued the practice of relaxing with their weekly visits to fill up with makale.

In the meantime, news had circulated that Japan and Russia had declared war over Korea. Japanese troops would land in Korea, their base of operations. One morning, Song noticed troops marching out of one of the ships. They were led by a soldier bearing the banner of a rising red sun on a white background. The soldiers wore dark blue uniforms with white trimmings and caps with visors. Each carried a rifle fixed with a bayonet as they marched to shrill orders given by a leader at their side.

The sound of their footsteps along the cobbled street was ominous to Song. He asked his friends if they knew what the troops were doing in Pusan. He was told they were there to ensure the independence of Korea from the Russians. The troops, they assurred Song, would bolster Korea's independence and Japan would serve as an advisor to Korea regarding international matters.

Song did not feel good with this answer. He was uneasy and had a sinking feeling in the pit of his stomach. Song had already become increasingly restless over the last six months. In fact, he had become quite curious about the world beyond the limits of Korea as he knew it. Earlier he had learned it was not possible for him to go to Japan as a worker. Peculiarly, the Japanese were bringing troops into Korea, yet he could not go to Japan to work! This was foreboding to Suk Soon.

He had heard about recruiters for laborers on sugar cane plantations in one of the territories occupied by the western giant, the USA, from the people at the Church. The territory was Hawaii, which sat far east in Tae-pyung-yang. They said that workers in Japan had been responding to such recruitement for a number of years, but that further recruitement of Japanese workers was being curtailed. Before the Japanese, the Chinese had been recruited before termination of their recruitment to limit the influx of Chinese into the USA. Seemingly, the plantation owners did not want a single ethnic group to dominate their labor force. Now, Korean workers were being recruited in great numbers, he was told. However, in the Korean case, members of the Presbyterian Church were taking a major hand in both their recruitement and their settlement in Hawaii, he understood.

Song thought seriously about a possible move across Tong-hae and Tae-pyung-yang to the new land. However, he did not have free time to seek information at the offices to which he had been directed by others.

One day shortly thereafter, he arose feeling alternately warm and hot and uncomfortably cold. He shivered visibly, alarming his housemates who advised him to remain in bed. They offered him miso soup and tea and promised to notify the boss about his illness.

Over the next two days, he continued to shake with chills and alternately run a fever. On the third day he felt better, but not well enough to take on the rigors of work at the dock. By the afternoon, however, he felt well enough to venture out. He walked to the office where the men connected with the church that had given him sanctuary earlier had directed him to for further information about working as a laborer in Hawaii.

Entering the door, he found several men gathered around a

table. Joining them, he was startled by the appearance of the man seated at the table. He appeared unduly pale, as if he had an illness much like the one he had been suffering himself. The man's hair was light brown, his skin was pale with brown speckles about his cheeks, and he wore no beard at all! Light colored eyes peered from behind a pair of gold-rimmed spectacles perched midway down a nose as large as a horn. Although he was sitting, the top of his head was at about the same height as the heads of the majority of the men standing around him.

To Song's surprise, the man turned his attention to Song, asking him if he wished to sign up for work in Hawaii, in a heavily accented Korean, of all things!

Momentarily startled, Song nodded his head and readily found the courage to ask three questions:

"How will I get there?"

"How long is the work for?"

"How much will I get paid?"

The man answered each query, responding in Korean. He said that travel would be by ship, which would take almost two weeks because the ship would have to stopover briefly in Japan before heading off to Hawaii across the Pacific Ocean or Tae-pyung-yang.

An immigrant worker was obligated to work at the plantation for one year and that during that period he would be paid in accordance with his work performance, depending on the assignment given to him. He assured Song that an honest day's work for six days a week for one year should give him enough to pay for fare back to Korea and sufficient money left over to purchase a parcel of land for farming.

Song liked what he heard. He agreed to sign up whereupon

he was questioned in detail regarding the date of birth and other biographical data. When the paper work was completed, he was sent to the health officer located behind a curtained area. There he was cursorily examined with his outer clothing off and at the end he was vaccinated against smallpox.

He was then instructed to stand before a strange looking device propped on three wooden legs. A middle-aged Korean man stood behind the device with a black cloth over his head. The man asked him to stand very still. Then without warning, the man squeezed a bulb instantaneously producing a bright light, frightening Song, who braced backward. The photographer laughed and assurred Suk Soon that he was only taking his photo, explaining matters in some detail to assuage the youth's concern.

Finally, Song was asked to sign the papers on the dotted line. He was told the ship he would take would be leaving at the end of December of the current year, 1903, only a month and a half away.

In the course of this venture, he was able to speak in light conversation with others who were also signing up. The men were all seeking a better life, seemingly suffering from hard times in their current lives. Some had families of their own and were trying to find means to include them in their journey to Hawaii. This was permitted only if their wives would also work on the sugar cane plantations. Otherwise, they were told, their families would have to stay back unless the worker had the means to pay for their travel. Of course, arrangements for them to sail to Hawaii could also be made later after they had earned enough to cover these expenses, the men said looking at the brighter aspects of these prospects.

He hurried back to his quarters and laid back on his pallet to rest. As he laid back, he began to review the past and his current and future status of employment. At last, the adventure continues, allowing him another opportunity to improve his living conditions, perhaps to strike a fortune! Who knows, he wondered?

He thought of his current friends and the steadiness of his income at the present job. But, there were definite signs of an ominous change with the troops coming in. He did not like the looks of things, anticipating possible difficulties with the Japanese in the future. Even though his companions were good friends now, their attitudes could change in the event of a takeover of Korea by Japan. He knew he could not ally with them in the event of any conflict between their countries. Considering all things, his move to Hawaii would avoid conflict here and allow him a new way of life, he assured himself.

The very next day, he gave notice to his friends and also to their boss. Everyone expressed regret on his choice to leave, but honored his decision.

His close friends held a fairwell gathering at their usual drinking spot the weekend before his departure. One by one, his friends toasted Song-san and wished him the best of luck, including the prospect of finding a lovely bride in the very near future.

On the day of his departure, several of his friends walked with him to the pier. Song had a small satchel holding his effects-all of his worldly goods, including Yong Soo's dictionary.

Documents were presented to an official guard (another American) at the bottom of the gangplank leading to the America Maru. The ship was quite a bit larger than the ones Song worked on from Japan. A flag of red and white stripes with a corner of white stars on a field of blue waved from its mast. The ship bellowed steam with a low airy tone, every now and then. The official instructed Suk Soon to climb aboard and seek quarters in steerage in broken Korean.

Suk Soon grabbed the shoulders of the closest of his friends before stepping back and bowing to him. He repeated this with each of his other comrades. Then he climbed up the gangplank, turning back a couple of times to wave to his friends by swinging his arm in an arc. Each of them also raised his hand in farewell to a good friend and comrade.

Other men were also boarding the ship, some carrying bags, others holding satchels. Soon the gangplank was lifted and the ship belched steam more loudly and frequently than before.

Song stood by the rail smiling with a genuine warmth he felt for his friends and waving farewell to his comrades by sweeping his arm overhead as the huge anchor was lifted from the water by two men who cranked the rope to which it was attached onto a roller. Slowly, the ship began to move out of the harbor. Song viewed the receding figures with a bit of sadness as the city of Pusan and the surrounding area grew smaller and smaller.

The ship proceeded southeastwardly. He turned his eyes to the open sea and prayed to Hana-Nim, "Please take us safely to Hawaii and watch over me. I am alone and have no one. Please, Hana-Nim, keep us safe from rocks and storms."

IS THIS REALLY PARADISE?

Steerage was no way to approach paradise. First of all, it was far down in the hold of the ship where light was in short supply, day or night. Only a few oil lamps lit the passage ways after sunset, but even fewer lit the large dank steerage hall making up the place of residence for the majority of the men. Only the few passengers bringing their families were quartered in the two smaller, equally dark and dank rooms at either end of the main hall.

The main room was crowded with men. There were a few pallets on the floor, but many more net-like devices hung between poles like hammocks for sleeping for the majority of the men.

Meals were brought in twice a day in two large pots along with bowls and spoons which they were obliged to wash with their ration of water sitting in an open bucket in one corner. The fare was a miso stew of vegetables, mainly cabbage, potatoes. and beans, which was meant to be served on rice gruel. Calorically, the fare would meet the daily minimum requirements for most, but little could be said for its palatability or esthetics.

Body waste was placed in chambers set behind a curtained

framed wooden panel and assignments for their disposal over the rail into the sea were made by the head Steward who came down to oversee things once a day.

Over the course of the time that it took to reach Hawaii, many developed sea sickness or diarrhea. This lent an indescribable alkaline odor to the fetishness that already pervaded the rooms and halls. Most of the occupants vacated the area, seeking refreshing air on the deck of the ship for extended periods of time. Fortunately, no major storms were encountered making it possible to spend most of the journey on deck, assuming space was available.

Each day, a man preached in their hall. He spoke of God and Jesus, Resurrection and the Ten Commandments. Song sat through them each time, listening with care.

Their journey had included a stop in Japan for a few days during which the passengers were not allowed off the ship.

Towards the end of the next week, land was spotted off in the distance. "Hawaii!" they all shouted as a hazy, purplish brown outline appeared on the horizon.

As the outline grew more distinct, it turned out to be a rather small island. Everyone seemed relieved the ship moved past it, presumably on its way to a more proper destination.

Another island appeared later, much, much larger than the first with tall mountainous ranges that seemed to stretch on and on. Surely, this must be Hawaii, they thought. However, the ship by-passed this one also, continuing on eastward.

Before long the horizon was filled with the blue sea again and the other larger island they had passed was no longer visible. The steerage passengers who thronged the deck began to wonder whether they were being taken elsewhere.

The murmuring and agitation of the crowd was the same with

each shipment of workers, thought the Captain. He sent the Steward to the crowd to inform them that their destination was next, the island of Oahu.

The Steward said to the crowd, "We go to Oahu, not those two smaller islands. Don' t worry. We' ll get there soon."

While the majority did not understand everything he said, his words were restated in Korean by the man who preached each day. Soon the crowd understood and calmed down. Everyone fixed his gaze on the horizon, straining to visualize a paradise in the distance.

Eventually, a light purplish brown image reappeared on the horizon. "Look, look out there. It must be Oahu," a few exclaimed.

Sure enough, the image of the island intensified and grew as the ship continued its move across the quiet Pacific Ocean.

Yes, Tae-pyung-yang was indeed the Pacific Ocean. Song had heard that Hawaii was located near the center of the upper half of Tae-pyung-yang. It had taken them nearly two weeks to cross only one half of the sea with a short stopover in Japan. He was only too glad to disembark here and not at the end of Tae-pyung-yang.

They landed on the island of Oahu at Honolulu, the largest city of the entire island chain on January 9, 1904. From there, most were to be transported by horse drawn cart to the plantation at Waipahu or Ewa on the island.

Workers from other ships would dock at Hilo on the island of Hawaii or at Kahului on Maui for work on other plantations, they were told.

Song sat beside other familiar steerage comrades in an assigned carriage drawn by two horses and looked about. The area around the dock was quite busy with people, horses and carts.

A group of fine buildings stood off in the distance, different in architecture and materials used than those he had seen in Pusan.

They traveled along a cobbled path made up of peculiar black rocks said to be made from lava. On the way to their destination, he saw the sea to his left separated from a long low mountainous range on the right by an extensive plain lush with green. It was a beautiful sight.

The air felt warm, strange for January. The foliage was unique with colors dotting the plain and bushes appearing to be still in bloom along the wayside they passed. Trees with long fronds and large odd shaped ball like fruit lined some parts of the road they traveled.

Unlike Korea, there did not seem to be any craggy hills to cross. Thus far, he saw no creeks and streams, either. Far off to the right, he saw vast areas of cultivated green extending as far as he could see. He could make out carts, horses and people moving slowly about. In some areas he saw scattered buildings here and there. Perhaps these were the living quarters and the cane processing sites, he thought.

The cart entered a smaller road and soon the horses came to a halt. Four other carts arrived about the same time. They all jumped off and gathered before a small building where the foreman asked them for their papers.

He collected them as he assigned teams of twelve men to each of five small shacks located behind the small building. He said they were to be fed by cooks who would deliver their meals by cart each morning and evening. They were told to collect food at breakfast to take to the fields and that work would begin at 6 a.m the next day.

And so, life in Hawaii was to start for Suk Soon, offering him another chance, away from the vexing arrogance of a brother whom he loved, in fact, but could not withstand. Most of all, he missed his Mother, thinking of her with love unfathomable and everlasting. His thoughts also turned to his friend, Yong Soo. He would remember him as long as he lived and would hope to tell him someday in Heaven about his adventures following Yong Soo's untimely departure.

SHIPWRECK

Years later, in the southern part of Korea, Chun was calculating the potential profit to his shipping and trading company with the last shipment of goods from Pusan to Shimonoseki across the strait of Tonghae or the Sea of Japan separating Korea from the islands of Japan.

He had organized the pooling of financial resources among five trusted friends and was the major contributor toward the building of a ship, which plied these waters for trading goods between Korea and Japan. Goods were purchased from markets in Pusan upon consignment from dealers in Japan.

The latest shipment to Japan included timber, granite and iron ore packed in the center of the ship's hold along with a menagerie of other goods including dried bulky vegetative materials tied in large bundles for commercial rope manufacturing and burlap sacks filled with large spools of delicate silk threads piled high at the opposite end. This particular shipment also included large baskets of sea shells for the manufacture of buttons, ornaments and the like.

Returning shiploads usually included copper goods, woven

silk and cotton fabric as well as preserved food items for sale to the many Japanese living in Korea since the turn of the century, especially following the annexation of Korea by the Empire of Japan.

With quick fingers, he moved the beads of his abacus creating a characteristic click-clack when the numbers increased. He peered intently at the sheaves of papers on his table, periodically moving his fingers from the abacus to trace out an item on the right along an imaginary line on the sheet to the precise number and cost per item on the left, as writing was from the right to the left in Korea. After tallying these numbers, he pulled out a bound notebook with the orders from the Japanese. A few more manuevers with the abacus and he was done.

They would show a handsome profit with this shipment. He would meet with his four business partners in the morning and present his findings.

Smiling, he thought of their success and the slow but continued accumulation of wealth they were experiencing in their joint venture. It was not too long ago when he had inherited his father's small mercantile business in Tongnae and turned it into a successful silk manufacturing operation.

His success with the business allowed him to send both of his sons to colleges in Japan to study. After annexation of Korea by Japan, Korean students were allowed to enroll in Japanese colleges and he could afford to do so.

The eldest studied in Japan without much of a focus, returned prematurely, soon after married a fine young lady and was now supporting his family on the salary he earned working for Chun. However, his son's ability to communicate in Japanese proved to be an asset in Chun's trade with Japanese outlets. Now he lived with his own family in a modest home separate from Chun.

His second son successfully studied pharmacy in Japan and was currently employed in the city of Yokohama as a pharmacist. Through arrangements that his wife, the daughter of Mr. Hong, had made, a bride had been found for him who was willing to leave Korea to live in Yokohama, where her husband might continue to work.

Chun also had two daughters, the eldest who married years ago and had a small family of her own living in another town nearby and his youngest child, Bok Pil, who was born nearly a decade before in 1896, when his wife was believed to be unlikely to bear another child. Now only she and his wife remained at home.

He had to be very choosy about a potential spouse for his youngest, for she was different, unlike other girls and women, Chun thought. Whereas most women seemed only interested in kitchen and household things, Bok Pil was curious enough about reading and writing that he had already begun to teach her himself. She was a good learner, indeed, and often practiced her writing, trying even to use the brush and ink to write on rice paper!

Chun completed his work and prepared to leave the trading and shipping office, which was located off the pier, facing the harbor at Pusan. He had sold the inherited mercantile shop in Tognae and invested the money in the trading and shipping business he spearheaded in Pusan.

His eldest son was conferring with another trader and Chun indicated to him that he was done for the day. So, off he sauntered to a carriage for hire to ride the few miles back to Tongnae.

Along the street near the office, a horse-drawn carriage driver, who was familiar with Chun, tipped his straw hat and greeted him with a few words. Chun boarded and they clattered along the road, which was partly paved and partly cobbled with stone.

They passed a number of sites, some covered with a shack, others opened from which steamy clouds of warm vapor rose and wafted with the movement of the air they stirred up during their passage. An odor of sulphur pervaded the entire area, emanating from the mineral waters that surfaced in small, slow jets here and there. Several signs designating the covered areas as bath houses could be seen and Chun indicated to his driver that he was to stop at the usual one.

Dismounting with a bound, he handed over more than the cost of the ride and bid the driver goodbye. It was Chun's favorite thing to do on a day like this-knowing he had turned over a nice profit and that the future looked rosier than ever.

He entered, spoke briefly to an attendant and proceeded to the men's section to undress. He emerged and immersed himself in the warm mineral bath while the caterer hung his clothes and arranged a towel for him to pick up later. Several other men were already in the bath. Chun recognized them and engaged in casual exchange over a number of things.

After several minutes, he left the bath, wrapped himself with the towel and joined others who were drinking sool (alcohol) and nibbling on dried squid. Several drinks later, he felt wonderfully elated and soon realized it was time to head for home. He dressed, bid his fellow bathers goodbye, paid his fee and left on foot. Walking somewhat wide-based, he did not weave and before long, he turned down a familiar lane.

The house was hidden behind a gate made of rocks overlaid at the top with sloping tiles. Opening the gate, he stepped into a wide courtyard where his youngest daughter, Bok Pil, and a neighbor friend of hers were jumping alternately at the ends of a plank laid across the middle of a rock with a flattened top.

Bok Pil' s pig tails flailed about as she jumped into the air. Her skirt or chima ballooned out revealing her bloomer-like undergarment.

The see-saw allowed each player to rise several feet into the air before landing and subsequently hurtling the other up into the air. The view beyond the gate was forbidden to young girls except on market days or special family escorted outings. The see-saw allowed them to peek beyond the gates without censure and had come to be a popular sport for women of a wide age range.

However, this did not appear to be their preoccupation as they laughed and giggled on being launched, apparently in shear enjoyment of the momentary sensation of flying each experienced.

Chun called to Bok Pil who signaled to her friend and then quickly hopped off the plank after launching her friend into the air. Myung Hee, her friend, landed safely and stepped off the plank as well, knowing it was time to quit.

Bok Pil ran to her Father and bowed down to greet him. She briefly turned and waved to Myung Hee and headed toward the courtyard of the living area of the house with her Father. The sound of the gate closing indicated her neighbor had also departed for her own home.

Mrs. Chun had already witnessed her husband' s arrival, Bok Pil' s response and the departure of her friend. She had arranged dinner on a low table large enough for all three to sit comfortably around it seated on flat comfortable cushions.

Tonight, dinner included pulkogi (barbecued beef), water cress namul (seasoned, cooked), seasoned bean sprouts, kimchee (pickled cabbage), fresh lettuce leaves to wrap these ingredients with rice, spicy condiments and a bean sauce soup topped with tofu.

Chun told his wife the good news of another substantial shipment of goods sailing off to Japan, which would allow them and their eldest son to have plenty enough for months.

The good news and joy that filled all three lasted all evening. Bok Pil went to bed and dreamed of someday riding on the ship itself across the wide, wide sea they called Tae-pyung-yang to view the world.

Early the next morning, Mrs. Chun awoke to find the sky to be unduly dark, portending a storm in the area. In a flash which lit up the courtyard, she rushed to move her charcoal brassier from the open courtyard to the eaves of the roof over her kitchen. She proceeded to prepare breakfast, expecting her husband to be arising before long. Bok Pil would probably sleep until just before breakfast was called, but that was just as well since she had been exercising rather hard with her friend recently, she thought.

Before her preparations were completed, both her husband and Bok Pil had awakened, freshened up and were already seated for breakfast.

"It looks like a stormy day. It could be bad at sea," said her husband, peering glumly at the sky from the veranda.

"Perhaps the storm is only passing close to Korea and not Japan. The ship should be deep at sea, away from our shores, making its way to Shimonoseki and should be safe," he said to console himself a short time later, still wearing the worried look.

The storm arrived, raged, and continued on for two whole days with high winds, lightening, thunder, and ceaselessly pouring rain.

Both days Chun went off to work under a large lacquered

paper umbrella, returning home under the same cover, still looking gloomy. He did not stop at the mineral baths. He brought home a bottle of Japanese sakke (alcoholic drink) and drank almost all of it the first evening of the storm without much supper.

The next evening he did the same.

The weather had cleared by the third day, but Chun continued to raise the paper umbrella over his head as he walked to and from work, not riding the carriage anymore. For several days after the sun had returned and the sky was blue again, Chun returned home under the umbrella with a new bottle of sakke, looking depressed and worried.

Bok Pil wondered why he seemed so strange and different, especially now that the storm was gone.

A week after the storm, Chun no longer went to the office. Instead, he stayed at home, gazed at the ceiling and talked to himself. When he ran out of sakke, he dispatched his wife to purchase more. He refused some meals, ate little at others, seemingly preoccupied and withdrawn from interactions with his family, except for his eldest son.

His son dropped in daily and exchanged a few words with his Father who seemed to attend momentarily before sinking back into depression. His son would depart with downcast eyes, each time bowing to his Mother, patting Bok Pil on the head, and leaving without revealing the nature of his or his Father's concern.

About a week and a half later, his eldest son appeared at the gate with the four other partners of the company. They were escorted into the main room where Chun sat moodily on the floor on a flat cushion, drinking Japanese sakke.

They announced that they had just received news that their

ship had hit rocks well short of Shimonoseki during the storm and had rapidly sunk off the coast of Japan losing all goods and personnel. News had just reached Pusan from the agent in Japan, who awaited the arrival of the ship to no avail and had to verify the ship's fate through the Japanese harbor and naval authorities. It had taken time to verify, but definitive evidence of such a disaster had been found in the straits of Japan and well before Shimonoseki.

Chun was devastated to find his worse fear had become a reality. Loss of the personnel, many of whom he knew and had recruited personally, was at the core of the most disturbing nightmares he had been experiencing the past two weeks. Without other means of communication from the trading outlet in Shimonoseki, he had to await news coming from Japan to him in Pusan via a written communique transported across the very sea that had destroyed him. The wait was interminable, but had finally arrived and it was devastating, totally devastating!

How could he face the wives and families of the men who were lost? Who would provide for them?

Several had children about the same age as his own second daughter and some were even contemporaries of his own two sons!

Yes, there were goods that were lost, but these could be replaced even though there was no cash available to do so in the foreseeable future. The capital investments made by his friends and himself were also lost. But that is what can happen in any investment project, he told himself.

It was the total loss of men on the ship and the effects on their families that grieved him. Nothing could replace those lives, he said to himself, over and over again.

While money could never compensate their families, he had

to do something. Well aware that there was nothing but his home left of any monetary worth, his thoughts centered around the impact of the loss of their home. He would have to labor again because what capital his home might have brought would no longer be available.

Chun hung his head down and beat his fists on the floor. "Aiggo, kun-il-na-ta! (Oh dear, a terrible tragedy has occurred)," he said repeating this over and over emphasizing the tragedy of the circumstance because of the loss of the ship's personnel.

After some time during which all agreed to the devastation of the circumstance and the injustice of fate, his partners departed.

Chun continued to bemoan the loss of the personnel, naming as many as he could by name. His wife tried to console him, to no avail.

Hours later, Chun ordered his eldest son to contact each of the families of the lost personnel and to promise to provide them with that amount of money the lost hand was to have received for the last tour of duty. He indicated their very home should be sold to cover this expense.

With that, he withdrew from further conversations and interactions except to nod his head one way or the other in answer to queries from his family. Over the following days he withdrew further and further into himself, refusing to eat while accepting only Japanese sakke and an occasional sip of honeyed tea from his wife.

Mrs. Chun spent the ensuing days tending to her depressed husband, cajoling him to forsake the sakke in lieu of soup and rice without much success. She saw that their monetary reserve had dwindled and she needed money to purchase staples when her eldest son and a magistrate appeared at the gate.

She was told that the house had been sold, indeed, as

ordered by Chun and she had to prepare to move to a smaller house in another part of town. Her son told her this was the only means whereby each of the families of the personnel who were lost could be compensated with money to match salaries for the fatal journey.

He explained the home he had was too small to accommodate his parents and sister, apologizing for this and ascribing it to his lack of foresight. Feeling badly about things, he continued to tell his Mother how sorry he felt, "Miyan-hamnida, Omoni, chum miyan-hamnida (Sorry, Mother, so very sorry)!"

There was nothing to do but to move. And so, the Chuns moved to a much smaller house surrounded by a mud-daubed wall without tiles on top.

By now Chun was weaker and had become quite gaunt in appearance. He took small sips of soup and tea, but could barely rise to care for his personal needs.

Finally one morning several weeks after the shipwreck, Mrs. Chun found her husband cold and unresponsive. "If anyone could die of depression, Chun would," she cried outloud as she wailed in great anguish.

He had died in his sleep after weeks of depression during which dreams of stormy seas and drowning men constantly appeared, withdrawing only to be replaced by images of grieving women and children whose faces often took on the likeness of his own beloved wife, sons and even his daughters, especially Bok Pil.

Apparently, the anorexia and dehydration and most likely a viral infection conspiring with his alcohol intake thrombosed vital organs sometime during his last hours leading to a permanent end to his nightmarish anguish.

The family interred Chun in a cemetary established by the

Presbyterian Church after a brief ceremony in the hall located across the waterfront market place in Pusan. Mrs. Chun had attended services and was permitted to have her husband buried at the cemetary located at the edge of Pusan near Tongnae.

A group at the church prepared Chun for burial, placing him in an unpainted wooden box. A wooden cross was afixed at the site with his name and dates of birth and death carved on it. His business associates, families of the personnel who perished in the shipwreck and more were there, including Myung Hee's family and other neighbors.

It was said that he was a fair and decent man.

Bok Pil, dressed in white, the color of mourning, watched wide-eyed, solemn and frightened. She wondered about her Father's comfort--so cold to touch and laid out in a box with a cover over which men shovelled dirt.

How could he rise when resurrection time was come? She had also attended church and believed that Hana-Nim's son, Jesus Christ, had been crucified by enemies, buried for three days in a tomb, but had risen from death.

She worried that her Father would not be able to uncover himself from the dirt piled on the coffin, let alone open the lid to the box.

These concerns were far easier for her to wrestle with than thoughts of immortality. Still, she grieved, crying softly, wiping her tears with one of her Father's large handkerchiefs her Mother had stuffed into the pocket of her chima before departing for the funeral.

These events had their toll on everyone. For Mrs. Chun, there was no means of support for herself or Bok Pil. She could not see her eldest son providing for two families--his own and hers for long.

She worked out an arrangement with her eldest son to acquire dry goods to sell at the market in a substall, that is, a small stand before a regular stall. Rental was substantially less and was paid to the renter of the larger stall. Her goods included silk fabrics woven by hand, threads of various colors and qualities, cords and braided loops, buttons, needles and pins, thimbles and other dry goods not carried by the larger store behind her.

Each day she went off to the market, returning later in the evening with her handful of coins besides the basket of unsold goods, which she balanced on her head and steadied with one of her hands. On certain days, she returned with foods she selected at other stalls, which she also piled into the basket.

Each evening Mrs. Chun returned to an increasingly quieter youngster, who tried very hard to prepare supper and maintain the household chores, trying desperately to help out in any way.

As a preteen, Bok Pil acquired skills rapidly, cleaning their small house, washing both dishes and clothes with water drawn from the community well, preparing dinner and even helping to braid the loops and cords for marketing during any remaining spare time.

She missed her friend Myung Hee, who lived on the other side of town, as neither of them was allowed to wander off to visit the other these days.

As dusk approached, Bok Pil would peer through the gate, watching for her Mother's return. She quickly learned to distinguish her Mother's form hurrying home with the basket of goods perched on her head, steadied with one hand.

Her Mother had a particular gait with toes pointed outward under her long white chima (skirt). She wore the boat-shaped rubber shoes so characteristic of this country. Her Mother's hair was parted in the middle with the sides drawn back and wound into a tight bun held in place with a u-shaped sea shell pin. Along the sides of her face, Mrs. Chun's hair waved a bit allowing renegade strands to escape from the rest of her hair that pulled back to the bun. Her short jacket with the tie in front was also white, the color of mourning which she was likely to wear the rest of her life, thought Bok Pil, who was now allowed to don her colored dress again.

With the passage of time, Bok Pil was permitted to join her Mother at the market every now and then. She was fascinated by the hustle and bustle of people searching for and bargaining for various things. Seeing the array of goods displayed in the nearby stalls was an enjoyable activity. However, the household chores and cooking still needed to be done and so these forays into the world were much too few and far-between for her.

On the other hand, fetching water was a daily chore which Bok Pil rather enjoyed. It required a walk to the town well, waiting in line for one's turn and drawing up one bucket at a time. The drawing bucket was lowered or raised by winding the rope to which it was attached around a rod with a hand crank. Raising the water-filled bucket was a might difficult and Bok Pil was frequently helped by obliging women waiting their turn. As she was unable to carry more than one bucket at a time back to the house, two or even three trips were often required. She took this opportunity to greet and chat with others, soon finding others like herself who welcomed companionship.

And so, the years passed and all the while Bok Pil grew into young womanhood gracefully, but sadly, as she missed both her Father and her Mother--one irreversibly to death and the other unfairly to circumstance. She wondered what the future held for her, believing all the while that her fate would be in the hands of Hana-Nim, who would look favorably on her.

ANOTHER SLIPPERY ROCK

When Bok Pil reached seventeen, a severe summer drought affected the southern regions of Korea. The water level at the well had dropped and continued to drop forcing one to step down into the well in order to draw water using another bucket tied to a hand held rope, which one had to carry. At the height of the drought, the rope tied to the bucket was clearly too short to reach the water level from the first two stone steps down the well. Bok Pil had to step down to the third step to draw water for a couple of weeks.

Much to everyone's relief, rain had finally come in generous quantity during the night. As she headed for the well, she wondered if the rain had raised the water level sufficiently to return to the use of the bucket at ground level. It was late morning and people were milling about the town square, many with lacquered paper umbrellas in hand should it shower again, as threatened by the rumbling of thunder in the distance.

Bok Pil stepped closer and saw that the water level had hardly budged requiring the usual three steps down to reach and draw up sufficient water for her bucket.

When her turn came, she hitched her skirt up with one hand to secure her vision for placement of her feet while holding the rope and bucket with the other hand. She had successfully navigated the first two steps and then stepped forward to reach the third step with her right foot as she released the hold on her skirt to grasp the rope on the bucket.

Suddenly, her foot slipped and she fell forward into the well with her bucket. She hit the the rocky wall of the well with her head and screamed.

Others around the well cried out, "Aiggo, toro-jita (Oh dear, she's fallen)!"

Women began to clamor and several descended the steps to reach her, but were unable to hoist her up.

Finally a young man stepped forward. He asked the women to vacate the stone steps at once. Quickly stepping down the steps, he reached for Bok Pil's floundering arms. He successfully grasped an arm and proceeded to pull her out of the water onto the lowest stepstone. Then without any difficulty, he carried her up the steps to the plaza surrounding the well.

Bok Pil coughed and sputtered, bringing out water which she spat out. Her braids and her dress were wrung of the water by several of the women hovering over her. Bok Pil was overcome by a swirl of emotions--embarassment, fear, gratefulness and anger at the occurrence of the accidental fall. Additionally, she was acutely conscious of her barefootedness, having lost her rubber boat-shaped shoes in the well.

She caught the eyes of the young man who had pulled her out and thanked him by bowing deeply several times without saying a word because nothing more could have better expressed her gratefulness to him for coming to her rescue.

He looked to see that she had recovered normal breathing,

smiled, stood up, politely bowed once, and then left.

The women around praised him as he walked away.

Shortly, they urged Bok Pil to return home to change into dry clothes and to return with another bucket for water.

As she walked back towards home, barefooted on the cobbled street, she considered the near drowning experience as somehow peculiarly almost even exciting. It gave her that sensation she had felt in the past while jumping up and landing back on the plank while see-sawing. Only not knowing that she would be saved by someone after the water interfered with her breathing, nearly choking her to death, pushed that sensation to one of panic. How strange, she thought!

Once home, she changed into dry clothing, laying out her damp ones on a line bridging the small courtyard. Amazingly, she managed to complete her chores in the house, cooking supper, and now was awaiting her Mother's return, anxious to tell her about the eventful morning. She had lost her shoes and had nothing to wear on her feet that would enable her to return to the well for water.

Her mind was swirling with the events of the day, not only the humiliation of falling into the well, the near drowning and her complex reactions to it, but also to the arrival of the young man who saved her life.

How handsome he was! So brave and strong! She wondered who he was and whether she would ever see him again. She prayed, thanking Hana-Nim for saving her from drowning through the intercession of the strong, handsome young man.

Watching for her Mother's return from a day at the market, she saw her familiar form sauntering slowly under a heavy load. Quickly, Bok Pil rushed to the door, opened it, and helped her unload the basket.

Unleashing her pent up story of the tumultuous day, she described the instantaneous fall, the near drowning, and her relief on being rescued. She told her Mother of the loss of her shoes and the bucket, and her inability to return for water.

As she was recounting these details, her Mother's face took on a most troubled appearance. Then, her eyes watered, followed by tears that trickled down both cheeks. She reached for her handkerchief in her skirt pocket and cried and wailed outloud, "Aiggo, aiggo!"

She reached for Bok Pil and hugged her, praising Hana-Nim for saving her. When she had calmed down, she assured Bok Pil that she would obtain a bucket of water and pick up a new pair of rubber soled shoes for her, forthwith.

Immediately, she left to do just that without a touch of supper. It was not long before she was back with both. She sat down with Bok Pil to eat her supper, but began the ritual of praying to Hana-Nim for all His blessings before reaching for her utensils. This ritual was to continue before each meal for the rest of their lives.

Mrs. Chun sought to learn the identity of the young man who saved her daughter from drowning. After some inquiry, she learned he was the son of a teacher, Moon-sobang (Mr. Moon), and was himself attending college to become a teacher. His name was Hyung Mahn and he was nineteen years of age. She related these vignettes to Bok Pil as she slowly acquired bits of information from friends and acquaintances.

Bok Pil kept these fact recorded in her mind and heart without revealing any emotions. She returned to the task of hauling water, apparently without fear. The water level was still low, but now she carried a cord to tie around her waist to hitch her skirt up maintaining clear vision all the way through the task of stepping down into the well. She was especially careful not to work with the rope and bucket until both feet were securely based on the rock.

Each time she went to the well she wondered whether Hyung Mahn might be in the vicinity. Although she wasn't sure what her reaction might be if she were to meet him, she hoped to see him again.

A couple of weeks later, she caught a glimpse of him only a short distance away from where she stood in line at the same well. He was hurrying along, but stopped momentarily after glancing at the group of women around the well. Bok Pil smiled shyly and bowed to him.

Recognizing her, he bowed in response, smiled and continued on his way.

Thereafter, Bok Pil saw him several times a week. Each time, she smiled and bowed to him and received the same acknowledgement in return. This was an experience that brought untold amounts of joy to Bok Pil who dreamed of life with Hyung Mahn as the best thing that could happen to her. Perhaps, she even thought, life together with Hyung Mahn could have been ordained by Hana-Nim and her unfortunate and frightening experience was the means for their introduction.

Mrs. Chun was becoming increasingly aware of a change in Bok Pil since her traumatic near-drowning episode. Instead of dread and depression, Bok Pil seemed happier, cheerier and fully ready to refill the buckets with water from the well without any urging. Slowly, Mrs. Chun came to suspect that Bok Pil had developed a romantic attachment to Hyung Mahn, which she readily understood.

She was also reminded that her daughter was nearing a marriageable age. While she could consult a marriage broker about Moon Hyung Mahn, she was well aware of his scholarly background and her inability to provide a suitable dowry following the loss of the family's fortunes both in business and personally. She wrestled with the dilemna and after consultation with her eldest son decided to engage a marriage broker to inquire about the eligibility of Hyung Mahn for Bok Pil and to negotiate a reasonable dowry.

As it turned out, Hyung Mahn's eligibility had been apparent to several other families with marriageable daughters including one who was acceptable to his parents, whose dowry was far more than Mrs. Chun could ever muster.

And so it was not long after that Hyung Mahn married another. Bok Pil heard about this, but evidenced no reaction in her Mother's presence. In reality however, her heart was broken. She wept when her Mother was away at work, beating her chest with her fists and sobbing on her pallet. She reconstituted herself before her Mother's return and kept up with her routine, never breaking down in her Mother's presence.

But, Mrs. Chun knew her grief and shared her sorrow without revealing her own awareness of these to her daughter.

Other opportunities for an arranged marriage arose, but none of the candidates was satisfactory to Bok Pil who cried and cried as each candidate's qualities and virtues were expounded to her by her Mother and the marriage broker. She consulted her sons and her eldest daughter. Each made suggestions of possible candidates, but none was acceptable to Bok Pil.

It was clear that Bok Pil would not settle for anyone they presented. By the age of 22, Mrs. Chun began to worry that her daughter might remain unmarried, a blight to respectable families and a sign of her failure as a Mother.

One day when Bok Pil was at the market helping her Mother

at her stall, a wife of one of the men who had died in the wreck of her Father's ship came by with her daughter, who was a few years younger than Bok Pil.

After the usual greetings and conversations, the woman told them that they were seeking silk cloths to prepare clothing for her daughter, who was sailing to Hawaii to be a picture bride of a handsome young worker. They learned that the Presbyterian Church and other Christian groups were extending the services of marriage brokers to the large number of young men who had crossed Tae-pyung-yang for work in Hawaii.

It was said these men were earning lots of money and that conditions in Hawaii were excellent. Those who could afford to do so were looking for suitable young ladies of a marriageable age to travel to Hawaii to be their wives. Details of the ages and family backgrounds and photographs of their appearances were available on these young men. The local church across the entrance to the market had such a service and held these documents with photographs of the men seeking appropriate brides. Instead of a broker who would expect a fee, the church served without expectation of such although donations to the church were accepted, they said.

After the sale of fabrics and threads to the Mother and daughter, they wished each other well and the buyers departed. The look of happiness in the young girl at the prospect of her coming journey to Hawaii to marry someone who was working and earning enough to pay for her trip did not escape Mrs. Chun or Bok Pil.

Mrs. Chun visited the service area of the church alone one day to view the documents and photographs of the men in Hawaii, who were willing to sponsor brides. According to the man who showed her several documents, a picture of the potential bride along with her documents would have to be acceptable to the sponsor, as well. This seemed fair to Mrs. Chun and reminded her of the work of any marriage broker with both parties in Tongnae.

With this information, she looked over the documents of a number of sponsor candidates. One in particular, Kim Sok Gun, looked very promising. He was the third son of a farmer who had received education enough to sign his name in hanmun or Chinese characters. Several years older than Bok Pil, he was stated to be healthy, of good size by height and weight measurements and had a strikingly handsome face by photograph.

That evening, Mrs. Chun confessed to Bok Pil that she had explored the picture bride program at the church. She talked about Kim Sok Gun, extolling his apparent education, family circumstance, size and his good looks. She asked Bok Pil to come along and to examine his record at the church. To Mrs. Chun's relief, Bok Pil agreed and did so the next day.

Bok Pil recognized the man behind the desk as a vestryman at the church. He talked about the program and showed her several of the documents of the men the church had approved to serve. One document caught her eye. It was the document with the picture of Kim Sok Gun. Just as her Mother had said, he was handsome indeed, and his background and dossier were very satisfactory. She was struck by his resemblance to Moon Hyung Mahn.

Instinctively, she blushed and said something to her Mother which led her Mother to ask the man what was needed to be done to become a bride for Kim.

There followed a series of questions as the man jotted the answers on forms which he had pulled out from a drawer. Bok

Pil was asked to sign the forms following which instructions were given for the delivery of the documents to the office used to recruit workers in Hawaii and for a photograph to be taken of Bok Pil at the same place.

Mrs. Chun and Bok Pil walked over to the designated office where the forms were inspected. Bok Pil's photograph was taken and they were advised to await a response from Mr. Kim, which could take several months. In the meantime, they were advised to prepare Bok Pil for possible departure to Hawaii should Mr. Kim Sok Gun agree to sponsor her travel to be his bride.

It did not take long before Bok Pil began to see a recurring image of someone with a broad smile fixed on her meeting her at a dock. He looked like Moon Hyung Mahn, but she would call him Kim Sok Gun. She wondered at the stated height of him. He would be taller than her by nearly a hand's length. Surely she thought, his shoulders would be broad, firm and strong. Perhaps he might even be able to lift her as Hyung Mahn had, she ventured in thought.

But, would she be able to cope in a foreign land?

She was told that the communities in which the men lived included other Korean families and Christian services much like theirs were available in Hawaii. With assurrances coming almost daily from others who had sent daughters to be brides based on document and picture exchanges with the church as a broker, Mrs. Chun prepared Bok Pil for the prospective journey.

Additional clothing including rubber shoes and stockings, a new blanket, but thinner for it was said to be warm all year round in Hawaii, lacquered chopsticks, procelain spoons and other lighter goods were gathered together to be tied in bundles for the possible journey.

Two months later one evening, the vestry man at the church appeared at their door. After greetings were exchanged, he produced a set of documents and announced that Mr. Kim Sok Gun had agreed to sponsor Bok Pil's travel to Hawaii to be his bride. The church had a set of documents for Bok Pil with a picture of herself on one sheet and a picture of Kim on another. She was then advised to be ready to sail on a particular date. With the business of her travel to Hawaii for marriage to Kim Sok Gun completed over honeyed tea, the vestry man departed with a bow and wishes for a happy life for the prospective bride.

CROSSING TAE-PYUNG-YANG, THE PACIFIC OCEAN

It was early in September when Bok Pil arrived at the pier in Pusan with two bundles of luggage. Her elder brother, her sister and her Mother accompanied her.

She had dressed in white on this occasion, in mourning for her departure from her family. Her hair was fixed like her Mother's, something she had begun to do several years before. Like her Mother, wavy strands of hair along the sides of her temple refused to be captured to be strapped and pulled towards the small bun in the back to be held firmly in place with a shell u-shaped pin.

Her Mother secretly handed her a small bag of amethyst and silver nuggets to use for exchange purposes. Hugging her youngest daughter tightly for an instant, she asked her to write as soon as possible, reminding her to address all mail to her brother's home.

Earlier, she had told Bok Pil of her intent to move in with her eldest son and his family. He had urged her to move into his home and to retire from work. He would care for his Mother, he promised.

Apparently, Bok Pil's coming marriage without the need for a dowry had relieved her of financial obligations and sale of the house made the amethyst and silver affordable.

Tears flowed down her eyes as Bok Pil said goodbye carrying her two bundles and walking slowly up the plank. She reached the top and found space along the railing where she placed her bundles down. She scanned the pier, found her family and waved goodbye to them intermittently at first, but with increasing vigor as the S.S. Hama-maru hooted loudly, announcing its departure. She sobbed softly to herself.

A matron with two young children was standing close by. She looked kindly at Bok Pil and consoled her saying, "You will return one day, don't be sad."

Her children, a girl around seven or eight and a boy around five or six, were peering through the railing bars and pointing to someone at the dock.

Bok Pil watched the receding figures, now waving without stopping except to wipe away her tears.

As the ship pulled out of the harbor and the figures were no longer visible, the matron about the age of Bok Pil's elder sister picked up one of the two bundles and urged her to follow her down the steps to the passenger hold of the ship. She had already situated her family's belongings in the passenger area she said, occupying two cots next to a third which lay unoccupied. She suggested that Bok Pil might want to claim the unoccupied one for herself and she set the bundle she was carrying down on the cot.

This was fine to Bok Pil, who was glad to know she would be situated next to a friendly and kind person. She graciously thanked the matron for her help.

The kindly lady was the wife of a Korean minister who had

sailed ahead to establish a church in Hawaii in one of the towns populated by a sizeable number of Korean workers and their families. She was traveling with their two children to join him. Her husband, the Reverend Lee, had been recruited by the Presbyterian Church in Korea and the U.S.A. for this service and had been away for more than half a year before the church sent for the rest of the family to join him.

Mrs. Lee was a warm person who was not only protective of her children, but extended these concerns to Bok Pil, chaperoning her to the dining hall, showing her the toilet facilities, and engaging her in conversation throughout the trip, while overseeing the care and management of her own active and inquisitive children.

The passenger hall was modest, filled with cots lined in rows for the women and children traveling without men. There were others only for men, she was told, and still others for individual families in the decks above.

Meals were served three times a day in the great hall where everyone gathered. Rice and soup together with pickled vegetables sweetened with malt as seemed customary with the Japanese were served with each meal with the addition of tofu or a rehydrated dried fish to embellish the protein content of some of the meals. There was plenty of water to drink as well as tea. Water was even available for washing bodies and clothes when one could get to one of the six trough-like sinks that were available in the bathroom area of the hold.

Bok Pil chatted with Mrs. Lee and helped to look after the two children. She showed Mrs. Lee the picture of her husband-to-be. Mrs. Lee admired his looks from the picture attached to Bok Pil's document. They talked about their past and the things they looked forward to in the future. Bok Pil's eyes welled up with tears when she told Mrs. Lee of her Father's death and the changes that had brought. She mentioned her fall into the well, but left out her feelings and disappointment upon learning of Hyung Mahn's marriage. The reason she gave for her unmarried status at age 22 was that each of the candidates her Mother selected was unbearably ugly. She could not conceive of living with any of those suggested. She did admit, however, that the dowry her Mother could raise left them little choice but to explore the church-supported marriage brokerage method for workers away from Korea.

These interactions and many other areas of mutual interest led to a bonding between Mrs. Lee and Bok Pil, who now called the minister's wife Hyung-nim, or big sister.

After a seeming eternity at sea most of which was in calm weather, early one morning the horizon began to fill with a purplish grey hue growing increasingly more distinct with time. There was a general buzzing in the hall and before long everyone began to gather his belongings and move towards the stairs leading to the deck.

It was early spring of 1919 when the ship made its way closer and closer to the harbor in Honolulu. The purplish grey had given way to lush green with a mountain seemingly sloping at one end into the sea while the other edge formed a short range, which people called Diamond Head.

There was a sense of great anticipation in the air. Everyone was on deck, watching a group of people on shore coming closer and closer into view. Mrs. Lee spotted the Reverend and pointed him out to her children and to Bok Pil, as the ship maneuvered into its berth.

Bok Pil searched and searched for the likes of Kim Sok Gun without success. She touched Mrs. Lee's arm and asked, "What if he isn't here for me, what shall I do?"

Then, she held her by the shoulders with both hands and said with a warm smile, "Don't you worry. If he is not smart enough to come for such a beautiful and loving bride-to-be, you can come home with us. We'll take care of you. We'll wait to make sure that your prospective husband has found you before we leave," she promised.

Bok Pil was relieved as she continued to search for a handsome Korean man, one who looked like Moon Hyung Mahn, but would be called Kim Sok Gun, the man with whom a new life would begin.

ENCOUNTER WITH FRAUD

The gangplank was laid and passengers decended toward an official who asked for documents at the bottom. One by one names were checked off a list that the official held in one hand as passengers were permitted to pass to the greetings of family members and/or relatives and friends.

Mrs. Lee and her two children preceeded Bok Pil, received clearances and rushed to the greetings of a middle-aged Korean man, the Reverend Lee, wearing a Panama hat and a blue-grey suit.

Bok Pil presented her documents and was allowed past. She looked for anyone resembling the handsome Kim Sok Gun depicted in her document.

Instead, a short thin man with pock marks all over his face emerged and bowed addressing her as Chun Bok Pil and introducing himself as Kim Sok Gun.

Bok Pil flushed, looked with bewilderment and spouted in rapid sequence, "You are not Kim Sok Gun."

"Who are you?"

"How do you know that my name is Chun Bok Pil?"

"Where is Kim Sok Gun?"

The short thin man with the pock marked face said that he was Kim Sok Gun and that he was her sponsor having paid and agreed for her to come to Hawaii to be his bride.

Bok Pil burst out loud, "No, no, no! You are not the Kim Sok Gun I came to marry. You are lying, you are a fraud!"

She searched furtively in the crowd for Mrs. Lee, the Reverend's wife. She spotted the matron and hurried towards her carrying the two bundles and calling frantically, "Hyung-nim, Hyung-nim, tora-jusaeyo (Big sister, big sister, please help me)!"

Pointing to the short thin pock marked man who followed her, she asked Mrs. Lee with great anguish, "How can it be? That man with the pock marks is not Kim Sok Gun!"

"Please, help me to find the man in the picture and save me from the man with the pock marks who claims to be Kim Sok Gun!" she pleaded.

Mrs. Lee said a few words to her husband while the pock marked man tried to wrest the bundles from Bok Pil, who hung on dearly to her worldly possessions biting her lower lip with her teeth.

"Get away from me, get away!" Bok Pil growled.

The Reverend came forward and kindly took the pock marked man's hands off the bundles. He handed them to his wife and asked Bok Pil to show him the immigration document with the picture of Kim Sok Gun. It was quite clear that the picture was not that of the pock marked man and neither were the physical dimensions listed of the man standing nervously before them.

The Reverend turned toward him, looked intently into his eyes and asked him what his *real* name was. The man replied that he was Kim Sok Gun, indeed.

"Then the picture you sent and these descriptions must belong to someone else, for you neither look like the man and you are certainly much shorter and weigh less than this man is supposed to, here in this legal document."

"Falsifying an official document is a criminal act, you know, for which you could be jailed."

"Who is he?" the Reverend continued, as he pointed to the face on the document.

Kim Sok Gun looked agitated and after shifting about a bit, admitted that a friend of his had posed for the picture while the physical description was made up.

With that the Reverend looked sternly at Kim Sok Gun, told him he would not take this up further, if and only if, Kim Sok Gun left the defrauded young lady alone. The Reverend said he and his wife would take care of her until she could find her way back to Korea.

Should Kim Sok Gun do anything to upset the young lady, he, the minister of the Korean Presbyterian congregation in the Waipahu and Ewa area would take the matter of fraud up with the immigration authorities. The consequences of fraud would be imprisonment and deportation back to Korea, he warned.

"Do you understand?" he asked raising his voice and frowning.

Kim Sok Gun seemed to shrink even further, nodded his head in agreement and promptly left the area.

Much relieved, but terribly shaken and disappointed, Bok Pil sat down on the nearest bench. Covering her face with both hands, she cried unashamedly.

Mrs. Lee came to sit by her, consoling her with gentle strokes of her hand across Bok Pil's arms and said, "We shall take you home with us and you can help me with our children for as long as is necessary."

A few moments later, Bok Pil stopped crying, wiped her face with her handkerchief and commented that fate had strange ways of dealing with people. Here she had fallen in love with a picture, not a real person and she was being punished for such a shallow approach to marriage. She vowed that the man she would ultimately marry would be selected in person, not through a figment of one's imagination, or through a picture.

She thanked Mrs. Lee for helping her and promised to help with the children and the care of the home until she could find the means to return to Korea.

BOK PIL CHUN (SONG),
picture on passport to Hawaii

PERSONAL  SELECTION

Bok Pil Chun went to live with the Lee's helping her "adoptive" older sister raise her family in a home rented by the Reverend Lee in the town of Waipahu near Ewa on the island of Oahu.

The town of Waipahu was situated in the midst of the sugar cane fields where workers from Korea, China and Japan worked to raise the tall cane plants, harvesting the fruitful stalks after burning the dried leaves for extracting and producing the crude molasses from the ground up stalks for shipment to refineries located on the continent of the U.S. where sugar was purified for distribution and sale.

Sugar cane plantations had developed on several of the islands of Hawaii and although Oahu was the third largest of the islands, the capital, Honolulu, was located here.

Honolulu was a major port city and therefore important to the plantation owners who stationed their main offices there. Waipahu was not too distant from Honolulu and a major artery had been paved to the port of Honolulu to facilitate commerce.

Both Mrs. Lee and Bok Pil marvelled at the differences in living conditions in Hawaii as compared to Korea.

Not only did the houses look quite different compared to houses in Korea but there were no gates surrounding them. Instead, a row of hibiscus (moogungwha) plants often ringed the house merging with other blooming shrubs scattered around the lawn of green. The house the Lees lived in had a few trees providing shade about the grounds. Several wooden steps led to a porch beyond which a door opened into the main chamber of the house.

There were five rooms altogether, the kitchen, the living room, two sleeping rooms (one for the Reverend and his wife and the other for the two children which Bok Pil shared), and a washing area with a step down to an outdoor pit with a seat, a convenience yet to be introduced in Korea.

Tables and chairs were available in the kitchen and the living area, although the family preferred to sit on flat pillows, both for meals and for leisure.

Oil lamps were only used when going outside of the house at night. Unlike Bok Pil's home in Korea where indoor lighting was dependent on oil lamps, an overhead glass bulb emitted light through electrical power. Each room had one hung in the middle, which could be turned on or off by merely twisting a switch above the bulb.

A wood-burning area for hot water to be prepared for bathing and washing clothes was just outside the wash room, separated from the pit. Clothes were scrubbed on a washboard in a large pan before hanging on a line set between parallel poles to dry outdoors, even now in the fall of 1919.

Reverend Lee explained the use of the kerosene stove with the three burners for cooking-a great convenience compared to the work involved in starting the burning pit used for cooking in the old country.

Water faucets were located over the sink in the kitchen and over a large tin pan in the bathing area. The flow of the cool clean water could even be controlled through the turn of the handle of the spigot itself. What ease compared to the work involved hauling water by the bucketfuls, Bok Pil thought outloud!

Ice was delivered twice a week for a box in the kitchen where food could be kept for a defined period of time, reducing spoilage. Daily shopping was thereby unnecessary.

It did not take them long to accommodate themselves to the many conveniences of the Hawaiian way of life.

Bok Pil helped with the cooking, the cleaning, and the care of the children. She even tended the vegetable garden and the chickens cooped up in the backyard. The gardening and chicken tending were novel activities for Bok Pil, but she quickly learned and seemed to enjoy feeding the chickens twice a day, gathering the eggs from the nests in the coop, as well as harvesting the different vegetables that had been planted in the garden by the Reverend.

Before long a number of unmarried men from the various work crews on the sugar plantation began to drop in to visit the Reverend and his wife, obviously eager to see the unattached woman with the "guts" to reject a fraudulent sponsor. News of her rejection of the pock marked sponsor became the talk of the Korean community and most people admired her for her courage. A few believed she might be an undisciplined hussey, provoking several to look her over with extreme caution.

Bok Pil regarded these visits with contempt, fading into the background when they occurred. Soon it became clear that she was indeed an honorable woman of courage who would not be fooled by the false documents of a sponsor and that she was certainly worthy of a fine husband, who had yet to be identified.

One day, Bok Pil was asked to walk over to the local plantation general store to purchase dried ginseng for Mrs. Lee, who had been suffering from excessive bleeding during her menstruation. She was unable to go herself because walking aggravated the bleeding and the store was further away than she considered wise for her to venture.

Bok Pil readily agreed to go. Since she was going to the store, she was asked also to bring back a few other goods as well, including a bag of mung beans, several blocks of tofu, dried fish and seaweed, a bag of rock salt and a few other items. She hurried to obtain the magical ginseng and the other goods, speeding down the unpaved dirt path to the plantation store with eagerness. She had never been in the store itself before, but knew where it was.

Once inside the store, she was surprised by the number of things on the shelves and counters, many in packages with attractive labels, as well as the barrels of goods on the floor. There was plenty to choose from but as she was in a hurry, she quickly asked for ginseng and the other goods, paid for them with the money given to her by Mrs. Lee and hurried to return to the house.

The goods had been placed in a large paper bag with the bulky excesses of several items sticking out obscuring her vision to some extent. She peeked around the bag to open the door and was making her way down the steps when she bumped into someone she had not seen because of the visual obstruction caused by the bulky items.

That someone caught her by the arm to keep her from falling down the steps. It was a man who said in Korean, "Careful, or you'll make us both fall."

He had noticed her long chima under the large package and the characteristic rubber boat-shaped shoes on her feet and knew she was a Korean woman. He laughed and allowed her to pass to the ground, all the while holding her by the arm to steady her.

She gasped out loud and apologized for her clumsiness.

The man insisted it was he who was at fault and followed this up politely with the suggestion that he could help with the package, which appeared unduly heavy for such a delicate woman. He had driven a company truck which was parked nearby and he would gladly drive her and the package to her home, he offered.

Bok Pil was surprised by this offer, but glad and relieved. She thanked him and released her hold on the bag, which had suddenly become unduly heavier than before.

The handsome, well-built and tall man led the way to a small truck parked nearby, helping her to the passenger seat. He laid the large package beside her and the driver's seat. Moving to the front of the truck, he bent down and rose up several times to crank and fire its engine. It fired up with a loud noise.

Before climbing into the seat, he reached into his pocket, pulled out a cigarette, lit it and puffed away. Hopping into the cab, he masterfully took hold of the wheel and pedals and began to drive the truck slowly down the road, following her directions to the house.

SUK SOON SONG, portrait taken later in life

Along the way, he told her his name was Song Suk Soon and that he was leading a crew of workers from the town digging a tunnel nearby and had dropped in to the store to pick up a few supplies. He would return to the store afterwards to complete his mission, he assured her.

She told him her name and the fact that she was staying with an adoptive sister, the Reverend Lee's wife.

Song told her he was from Chongsong in Kyongsang-pukdo and Bok Pil countered she did not know where that was as she had lived in the Tongnae area near Pusan all her life. They continued to talk about their individual home towns in Korea like old friends, totally unlike the behaviour of an unmarried young lady and a man in Korea.

A few minutes later, they arrived at the Reverend's house as Song rubbed the stub of his cigarette against the stained dashboard and placed the smoldering remains into a small tin can on the floor next to the hand brake.

Mrs. Lee appeared at the door, on hearing the truck approach.

Song introduced himself after Bok Pil explained how she had nearly knocked him down the steps to the store, because the package had obscured her vision.

Mrs. Lee laughed at the story as Song carried the package into the kitchen.

After a brief chat over a cup of tea, he left but promised to return upon Mrs. Lee's invitation for him to attend church services followed by lunch at her home the following Sunday.

Bok Pil could hardly believe the sequence of events that had taken place. She saw his face and heard his voice in her mind's eye and ear, ruminating over the events and the promise of another meeting to come very soon. She glowed and appeared cheerier than her usual affable self throughout the rest of the week.

This did not go unnoticed by Mrs. Lee, who told her husband about her adoptive sister's recent experience and the charm and handsomeness of Song-sobang (Mr. Song).

Song returned on Sunday driving the same truck from the outskirts of Honolulu, where he apparently resided, to attend church service and visit the Reverend's home afterwards.

Bok Pil was not the only one intrigued with Song. Both Reverend and Mrs. Lee found Song to be engaging and interesting, too.

He was nearly 36 years of age, had never been married and had arrived in Hawaii at the age of 20. When queried, he explained that he had come to Hawaii to seek his fortune. He was raised in a farming community. He said his Father had died and his Mother continued to live with his married brother who ran the farm. He gave no other details except to tell them that he had worked as a common laborer for the Sugar Cane Plantation for the year of obligation, and had then been offered a job as a leader of the group that checked out the water system for the fields before moving up to driving groups of workers to the various work sites after he had been taught to drive a truck.

He was then consigned to the plantation warehouse to pickup and deliver equipment and implements to the various fields, to transfer items between the piers and markets in Honolulu to the Plantation owned stores in Waipahu and Ewa. He had recently come upon the new job as head of a digging crew.

He had recruited the men he had known in Waipahu and had negotiated their work terms and salaries with the company responsible for digging the tunnel.

As he talked, the Reverend could see Song had leadership qualities and winning ways. Why would't other men follow his directions, especially for pay?

Song's interpersonal and intuitive skills were the major factors leading him from being a sugar cane field laborer through a progression of upgraded jobs to the present one.

Now, he directed the gang in their excavations, directing the movement of wooden struts to support them from cave-ins. While volcanic on the surface, layers of rocks of iron ore abounded and had to be picked to boulders that could be managed. Working with picks and shovels with the occasional help from a coal-burning steam shovel to clear some areas, long hours were spent digging in the dark, mostly with kerosene lamps lighting limited areas. Crews piled the dirt and rocks in a central area for the steam shovel to load onto carts for removal. The work was hard and depended largely on immigrant men who had completed their year on the plantations and who wanted other higher paying jobs.

Several native Hawaiian men also served in this capacity, he said. They were decidedly larger and stronger than the Asians in his group and therefore seemingly an advantage to hire. However, the several who had been hired tended to be unreliable, he said, frequently not showing up for work for one reason or another, especially after pay days. More than likely, he continued, those men over indulged themselves with alcohol for they tended to complain of symptoms of hangover for a couple of days after such episodes.

In spite of the fact that he worked underground, his skin was tanned. He wore his hair trimmed short, sporting large, well-formed ears. He was tall and handsome with broad shoulders and strong arms. His smile was especially engaging displaying white, beautifully set teeth.

Song glanced at Bok Pil who sat demurely by looking at him

every now and then without saying much.

After lunch was over, the Reverend took Suk Soon outdoors to look over the vegetable garden while the children romped in the yard.

The two women cleared the table and prepared tea.

Song took out his package of cigarettes and proceeded to light and smoke one after the Reverend declined his offer to help himself.

The Reverend told Suk Soon the story behind Bok Pil's arrival and stay with them.

Suk Soon laughed and exclaimed, "So, this is the little lady with courage who refused to be taken in by fraud that everyone had been talking about, eh?"

"Why, she is lovely! I would be honored to have her as my bride, if she would have me! I really wonder if she might consider me as a possible husband," he inquired.

"After all, she has seen me in the flesh already. I would be a good husband, especially as she has already made my heart throb since I first met her when she nearly knocked me off the steps of the general store."

"Saving enough money to return to Korea would take long, especially for a woman, and then she would have to go through another process of marriage brokering."

"I am unmarried, poorly educated but employed and I am of good health in body, mind and spirit," he said.

The Reverend could not believe what he had just heard. Quickly he asked Suk Soon not to follow through with any further inquiry just yet and to allow himself and his wife to approach Bok Pil for him. "You would not want to be rejected outright, do you?" he asked.

"We'll have to discuss matters with Bok Pil and see what she thinks of settling down with you as opposed to anyone else, or returning back to Korea."

"You know several suitors have come by already only to be soundly rejected by this sweet, but head-strong, young lady. And, my wife would not tolerate anyone forcing his wishes or another's on her. She is committed to having Bok Pil find the right man," the Reverend said.

Song agreed, but he now wore a twinkle in his eye, struck by finding the damsel with the courage to hold her own about whom he had heard and wondered. And, finding her here, now, and so attractive!

They returned and sat down for tea and fresh mango.

As she sipped her tea, Bok Pil peered behind her cup at Suk Soon. He was looking at her also with eyes that nearly glowed with pleasure at seeing her face.

Both were clearly taken with each other and the Reverend was sure there would be no difficulty about a match between them.

It was time for Suk Soon to leave. He promised to return the next Sunday at the Reverend's invitation, which was offered with a gentle squeeze of Song's forearm.

Bok Pil felt a rush of warmth as she blushed at the thought of seeing Song again.

Soon after Song was out of sight, the Reverend called his wife to their bedroom. He discussed Song's interest in Bok Pil and his assessment that Song was a good candidate for her.

He asked if his wife thought Bok Pil might consider Song to which she replied, "Ahh, yes, I think this is the right man for her. Did you not see their delight to be in each other's presence? Why I haven't seen Bok Pil in such a happy mood since the morning just before our arrival in Hawaii!"

They emerged from their room and found Bok Pil scrubbing the kitchen sink diligently even though it was spit spot clean already. They asked her to come out to the living room, where they sat on cushions on the floor.

The Reverend went straight to the heart of the matter and said that Song Suk Soon was interested in her as a bride and they thought he would be a fine husband for any daughter of theirs. They wondered whether Bok Pil would consider him as a possible husband.

To their surprise and pleasure, Bok Pil smiled and shyly agreed that she thought he would make a fine husband, too. She was willing to be his bride and was glad that the Reverend and Mrs. Lee were in agreement.

On that note, the Reverend proposed to get in touch with Song before Sunday so as to arrange a marriage ceremony at Song's earliest convenience.

As soon as Song was informed of Bok Pil's agreement after the Reverend had contacted him through one of the men who worked with him but still lived in Waipahu, Song dropped in to see them, again.

He grinned from ear to ear and suggested Sunday a month later would be a fine time for a marriage ceremony. He would arrange to be off from work one day each week to seek and prepare a proper home for his wife. As it was he was staying at a rooming house on the outskirts of Honolulu, but he knew of a house for rent in the area.

Furnishing could be done gradually as long as the essentials like pots and pans, dishes and bedding were available, he indicated, and these could easily be bought with the money he had saved.

He already had a phonograph, an RCA Victrola as well as a

number of ceramic records of western singers which he played often on his days off, he said. He hoped Bok Pil also liked vocal expressions of human feelings. This was his only personal possession of worth, he told them, but dividends from his investment in the machine were immeasurable. Someday, he hoped to hear his own children expressing themselves through a lyrical venue, he said.

The first Sunday a month later, after the usual church service, Suk Soon and Bok Pil were married by the Reverend Lee.

Bok Pil was dressed in a green silk chima with a pink jacket. She wore the traditional Korean pointed toe stockings and the boat-shaped shoes. The pin in her bun was decorated with designs and she had powdered her face.

Song wore a western cut suit of grey, a white shirt topped with a modestly colored tie which he had proudly tied himself. His black shoes were also western and made of leather.

The ceremony was Christian with each swearing to love and cherish the other till death did them part, all repeated in Korean. No rings were exchanged. There was no music and only a single candle burned on the altar before which they stood. They held each other's hands together as the Reverend blessed them and wished them a happy, godly life together.

Several friends of Song were in attendance beside Mrs. Lee and the two children.

After the ceremony, lunch was served by Mrs. Lee. Everyone ate and shared in the joy of the marriage. Bok Pil's belongings had already been taken to the rented house in Honolulu--a small structure with a slanting front porch covered with a rusted, galvanized tin roof.

After the meal was over, the Reverend blessed the couple, branches of hibiscus flowers were handed to the bride and the bride and groom left the Lees and their other guests holding hands walking together toward the truck that belonged to the company Song worked for. One of his Waipahu workers worked the crank of the truck. It sputtered and rattled. Song pressed his foot on the gas peddle and pulled the throttle out. The combustion chamber took off creating energy sufficient to drive the shafts and the bridal couple was off amidst waves and goodbyes.

They traveled along the dirt road creating a curtain of dust until they reached the main highway where the road was paved and then headed towards Honolulu. The afternoon sun was glowing, but a trade wind kept the couple cool. The rattling of the truck and the roar of its engine did not disturb the couple as they traveled along.

The bride marvelled that her husband could maneuver the mechanical beast as well as he did. Off to the right, she saw Tae-pyung-yang, the Pacific Ocean. She said something to the groom which he could not hear over the noise of the engine. He called out loudly to her that the sea was called the Pacific Ocean in the west, but that it would forever be Tae-pyung-yang to him. Bok Pil nodded her head in agreement, sharing his sentiment and feeling even closer to her husband than before. Both recognized their destinies were now linked forever through the commonality of having ventured to cross the mighty Tae-pyung-yang alone without any promise except that things would change, which they had already.

They reached their rented house and set the truck in front on the street. Entering the house together, they embraced and held each other tightly for a moment or two. Life together was to begin at this place for them and they would do the best to work together to improve their lot in pursuit of a common dream each held individually before leaving Korea, which they now shared. The individual circumstance peculiar to each would soon be revealed to the other over the coming days, weeks, months and years, strengthening their belief in the power of the almighty Hana-Nim who must have ordained their finding each other for a purpose.

THE EARLY YEARS TOGETHER

The bride and groom were as happy as could be living and loving each other in their small rented house. They had few material things, but there was little need for more as they discovered the joy of having found each.

The bride showed off her culinary skills, preparing special dishes for her husband, some he had not tasted in a very long time. He complimented her at every meal, exclaiming the dishes to be delicious. He talked about a traditional dish of the region of Kyongsang-puk-do which was a favorite of his, steamed chicken. She had never heard of the dish and could not see anything special about steamed chicken, she said. However, she would inquire about it and might prepare it some day, she assured him.

He enjoyed the fuss she made of laying out his clothes, straightening out the wrinkles in his clothing, picking off the dust balls here and there and readying his shoes whenever he was about to do so for himself. Periodically he would grab her by the shoulders and hug her tightly. Each time she melted in his arms for a moment or two before pulling back in mock modesty and spurring him on to continue with whatever he had been doing.

Of course, they had the Victrola and Song introduced his wife to it's use and the treasures that it could reproduce. It stood waist high on the floor and had to be manually cranked to finish one side of a ceramic record spinning at 72 revolutions per minute. Records could be stored in the cabinet below the turntable and sounds emanated from a separate speaker through a bullhorn located beside the turntable. After cranking the turntable to power, the phonograph was started by turning a button and swinging an odd, almost S-shaped copper arm almost 180 degrees to place its head above the record, carefully aiming the tiny, removable needle set in the head to the starting point on the revolving ceramic disk. Suk Soon played his favorite records sharing his modest collection with his wife. She listened to the new tones of the western songs with patience, commenting on her inability to comprehend the words.

The several records the groom had collected included operatic arias by Caruso and Madam Schumann-Heincke. He had purchased these after hearing them during the demonstration at the dealer's where the Victrola was bought. He also owned several records of traditional Korean instruments and chanting in the familiar tremulous manner that Bok Pil had heard before.

"How much sadder the tones of the Korean chants are compared to the western songs," she'd often comment.

Song noticed that she neither sang nor chanted as his Mother had. Still, she did appreciate Korean music, and that was just fine.

He also had Yong Soo's dictionary which turned out to be extremely helpful when reading an occasional book he was lucky to borrow from one of his acquaintances. Looking up the meaning of a Chinese character in the dictionary helped him to review the few characters he had learned long ago in Chongsong. He proudly showed his bride the dictionary and even demonstrated how to look up the meaning of a few words.

Of course, Bok Pil was filled with admiration at his ability to do just what her own Father had done whenever he was reading throughout her childhood.

Several days after their wedding, one of the men of the digging crew pounded on the door before day break. "Song-san, we need you to stake out the digging route today," he called.

Song called back that he would meet them at the site at 9 a.m the next day. So, after only a few days, Song went back to leading his crew in their back-breaking dig in the tunnel.

Each morning he left before dawn, taking a "bento" or rice box topped with spiced vegetables and meat, chicken, fish or tofu for lunch, which his new bride readied for him.

Each evening he returned after dusk, all dusty and tired. But after a quick rinse, he was lively and ready to speak to and love Bok Pil.

In due course, there was enough earned for them to slowly acquire a few pieces of furniture.

Bok Pil kept herself busy with the cleaning and cooking. She also purchased fabric of various kinds and began to sew things for the home and her husband, including pillows, covers, pajamas and underwear. She was quick and nimble with her fingers and Song came to admire her skill and execution with each of her projects.

She got to know her neighbors and found a neighborhood store where goods could be purchased for a reasonable sum. She was quickly adapting to western ways and already could speak and understand words and simple sentences in English, Hawaiian, and Japanese.

After a couple of months, Bok Pil noticed her menstrual period failed to come. She guessed she was pregnant and discussed the matter with one of her neighbor friends.

Shortly thereafter, her projects took on a different dimension. Now she cut out clothes too short and too small for Suk Soon. He eventually recognized she was preparing for a baby, which brought delight to his heart. Yes, she was to bear his first child and he was grateful to Hana-Nim for his wife's fruitfulness.

The house they had rented was a shack in fact, not close to other Korean families and rather far to walk to purchase merchandise for their daily needs. Suk Soon looked for and found a house for rent in Ewa where many Korean families resided with handy access to a local store. It was easy to move for they had few household goods, but they arrived with an overabundance of happiness, for did they not have each other and wasn't the fruit of their love growing and ripening?

Ten lunar months later, she went into labor. A local woman who served the community as a mid-wife was called in. She and the neighbor friend worked with Bok Pil, sending Suk Soon away from the bedroom where the baby's arrival was under way.

After many hours of labor, Bok Pil delivered a tiny, healthy girl. The baby cried pitifully and hard. Bok Pil's love for the newborn led her to reach and hold her despite the pain of the lacerations below. The placenta was removed and the blood and amniotic fluid were sopped up with cloths and wrung out by the two ladies. Soon order had been restored and the baby cuddled in her Mother's arms and slept.

Song was permitted in. He clutched his wife's arms and looked into her eyes. He smiled at his newborn daughter and said, "She is very well-formed, tiny but beautiful! We'll call her Hae Sun or Sea Fairy, if that is agreeable with you, my dear wife."

She, who was called Bok Pil, Wholly Blessed or Good Wishes, agreed and was overcome with love for the baby in her arms and its Father, the Pure, Solid or Kindly Rock, kneeling at her bedside.

Hae Sun waxed and grew, drinking from her Mother's breast, sucking until her hunger was quenched, then falling asleep for a bit, then waking to find the nipple gone at which point she would holler for its immediate reappearance to satisfy the fleeting but unendurable pang of hunger that she felt.

"Undoubtedly," said the Father on such occasions, "She has to be fed, immediately. You mustn't starve my beautiful Sea Fairy!"

Hae Sun quickly learned to turn from her back to her tummy and the other way around, bringing delight to her parents.

The Rev. and Mrs. Lee and their children visited and Hae Sun appeared to recognize them, too. She would smile at their cooing and look from one to the other. Everyone was impressed with her growth and development and soon she was beginning to sit, then to crawl, speak single words, and finally to stand.

Meanwhile at work, they were reaching the half-way point in digging the next tunnel and were bent on completing the job before the tropical storms would intrude almost daily during the fall in this climate. Everyone had worked hard, a large pile of rocks and dirt had accumulated for removal, and the men were moving their supporting timbers to a new site.

In the process of setting them up, one of the men lost his balance causing one of the logs to knock an adjoining one down. The impact of the drop caused four others that had been propped up to lean precariously towards one side blocking the entrance or exit way. The men shouted and hollered for help hoping to gain the attention of the men working outside. No evidence of help was discernable. By now dirt and rocks had fallen, filling and blocking the path to the entrance or exit way. Panic gripped the men as they began to claw their way toward the exit.

Song shouted for order and pointed towards one corner of the ceiling of the cave through which light could still be seen. Clearly, there was an opening to the outside and air was coming in even though the opening was beyond their reach, nearly 20 feet or so away. It would continue to supply air, he assurred them. He counted the men to be sure that everyone was accounted for. Indeed, all nine were present and uninjured.

Quickly, he had them organize a series of layered rocks starting with a base of larger rocks, raising each layer by another set of rocks, encouraging them to keep calm while building the staircase tower.

They labored for hours. There were plenty of rocks to use in their indoor construction and air was clearly coming through the vented ceiling of the cave where they were trapped.

Finally, Song climbed up the steps to the very top of the stone mountain they had built. It was a bit of a stretch to reach the opening and to squeeze himself through, but he succeeded. He called down to his men to follow him. They did so individually with help at the top from Song and those who succeeded him to haul out the next one in line.

At the end, they cheered each other with muted voices and exhalations of relief, slapping each other on the back and smiling, thankfully. They walked towards the main group of men of the project gathered a distance away to report their experience and self-rescue.

Everyone of the men thanked Song for using his head and showing them how to handle themselves in their most recent threatening dilemna. Each vowed to continue to follow Song through thick and thin, as one by one the men came over to Song to thank him for his leadership by patting him on the shoulder.

Song, on the other hand, announced that in view of this experience, he believed that his God, Hana-Nim, was advising him to seek another, less threatening way of life for the sake of his child and wife. So, he said that he would not return to lead his crew again and wished them the best with whomever was selected as their new leader.

The men tried to cajole Song into staying on, but Song held firmly to his decision to leave this line of work. He would speak to the boss in the morning, he said and left the men in friendship wishing them all continued safety in their work and a fond "aloha".

Song told his wife what had happened, but had not yet told her of his decision to leave excavating as a job when she burst out crying, "Oh my, oh my! It was Hana-Nim who has preserved you!"

Before he could respond, she immediately begged him to quite that line of work and to seek another one. She blurted further with her voice cracking that she would be more than happy to sew for a living if he could not find another job. There was no way that she would allow him to work digging tunnels anymore, she insisted with tears now streaming down her face.

In fact, she told Song, she had a little bag of amethyst and silver nuggets that her Mother had given her upon her departure for Hawaii. She had hidden it until now for a rainy day and now was willing for them to live on it until he found a new, safer occupation, or could set himself up in some sort of enterprise.

He had foreseen the likelihood of this sort of a reaction of alarm from his wife during the crisis in the tunnel. Calming her down, he told her he had already intended to leave that line of work, and had, in fact, resigned before his return home from work. He assurred her that he would seek another form of employment, or better still, check on a business possibility within the next several days.

Some time earlier, Song had heard the military had expanded their base at Schofield Barracks near the town of Wahiawa, not too far from Ewa. He knew that a number of Koreans had received concession rights to open tailoring and uniform laundering shops at Schofield. He had been considering seeking such a concession as a business for himself for some time. People could be hired to do the tailoring and the uniform laundering, even if he did not know how to execute these jobs himself. Now was the time to do so.

Following up on this intent, to his surprise, a congenial Colonel in charge of arranging such concessions for the 13th Field Artillary agreed to allow him to occupy space in the building assigned to his outfit for just such an enterprise. After signing the required papers, Song was shown the site located on the first floor of a large two-story concrete complex housing various components of the 13th Field Artillary Division. Soon after, a sign designating Song's Tailor Shop was posted above the door, through the courtesy of the Colonel.

The Colonel provided the necessary tables and counters for the concession while Song used his wife's precious stones and silver to purchase a sewing machine that was operated by foot power. He also purchased coal-heated irons, ironing boards, and other necessary tools for the tailoring and laundering aspects of the business, including hangers and clothes racks.

About this time, Song had an opportunity to buy a used

automobile from one of his former bosses, who was purchasing a sleeker, better looking, newer model. The automobile was a covered sedan which ran on gasoline and had to be fired up by a hand crank, like the truck. By far, the stick shift of the automobile was far easier to handle than the shift on the truck, he found.

The car would be necessary for his new business enterprise and would allow Song to commute from their new place of dwelling. Together with his wife, they had selected a new site to move to at Castner Camp just at the outskirts of the town of Wahiawa, next to Schofield Barracks, where many other Korean families lived.

Song also hired a fellow Korean man, who knew how to tailor, and a young Japanese man, Jimmy, who was to help with the laundering of the uniforms and in the management of the shop.

Initially the laundering of the khaki shirts, trousers, ties and caps was done on the bank of a river located just at the outskirts of Wahiawa. Starting early in the morning, he and Jimmy hand scrubbed the clothes using a tub and washboard, wringing them out by hand before coating them with starch prepared by his wife. The clothes were then wrung out again and hung on the bushes around the area to dry. They were gathered up around mid-afternoon, whether they were dry or not, to be pressed at the shop using coal-heated irons. On rainy days, the clothes were gathered and brought back to the shop for drying indoors, draped on hangers hung on the racks.

It did not take long before business picked up enabling Song to engage the services of a fellow Korean to wash and dry the military uniforms at the employee's home on a fee per piece basis. The ironing was continued at the shop by Song and his assistant. This process was more cost effective, allowing him to be present on the premises for most of the work day, while increasing their total work capacity in handling the increasing amount of clothes that had to be processed.

All appeared to be progressing well and before Hae Sun was a year old, his wife was pregnant again.

She went into labor at home with a local mid-wife, who was Japanese, and one of their Korean neighbors helping with the delivery of the baby--a healthy, large boy.

Song was delighted.

Using a spring weight, the midwife had placed the baby in the pan and announced that he weighed over nine pounds. Song nearly burst with pride! Imagine, more than nine pounds at birth! Why, he was nearly one-half the weight of his year old sister, he said.

Together they agreed on the name for their firstborn son to be Hae Jun, or Great Man of the Sea.

The baby waxed and grew, sucking hard at his Mother's breasts. His sister had been successfully weaned as soon as the Mother became pregnant again.

Late in July, nearly six months after his birth, Hae Jun caught a respiratory infection. He was fussy and was warm to touch. His appetite seemed to have abated somewhat his Mother thought, as each feeding period became progressively shorter. His sister had the sniffles too, but was not warm to touch, and she continued her usual intake of food.

Song believed a visit to the local doctor in Wahiawa might be helpful and convinced his wife to take Hae Jun to see him. His sister was also brought along on this visit.

The doctor was a pleasant man who examined the baby as well as his sister and gave his Mother a bottle of liquid medicine with a dropper and instructions to offer the baby a few drops every several hours. He said the baby had a bad cold, but would respond to treatment and no other instructions or precautions were given. On the other hand, he said, the baby's sister seemed to be weathering the respiratory infection quite well and that nothing needed to be administered to her.

Back at home, Bok Pil did the best she could to get some of the mucus out of the baby's nasal passages by twisting the end of a handkerchief and trying to dab the mucus blockage out. The baby had taken the prescribed medicines, but he continued to feed poorly.

He slept in a cradle beside his Mother's bed, which had allowed her to rock it from time to time to lengthen the time between feedings before the present illness.

This evening, however, he did not fuss and she thought it best not to waken him to feed. She quietly walked around to her daughter's crib against the wall near the window. Seeing that she too was asleep, both parents went to bed and slept through the night.

While it was still somewhat dark and only beginning to lighten in the morning, the Mother awoke before her husband. A peculiar sense of dread arose and grew in intensity when she noticed that the room was unnaturally quiet. She listened carefully and heard her daughter's quiet breathing, but the baby's noisy breathing of late was not audible at all. Perhaps his nostrils cleared from the medication, she thought. She reached for the cradle and rocked it gently.

The baby neither stirred nor made a sound.

Immediately, she rose from the bed and reached for her baby with both hands only to find a cold rigid form under the blanket in the cradle.

"Yobo, yobo (Dear, dear), wake up, something is wrong with

Hae Jun," she cried out in a loud whisper hoping to avoid waking her older child.

"What's wrong?" he asked.

Quickly jumping up, he peered at the baby in the semi-darkness of dawn, reaching with his arms to touch him. His fingers encountered the semi-rigid coldness instead of the soft warm body of his son that he had come to expect and loved. Realizing that something dreadful had indeed happened, he was frantic.

Now Bok Pil picked the baby up and held him in her arms, close to her breasts, trying to warm him with the warmth of her own body. Then, she placed the baby on the bed to look for spontaneous movements. Seeing none, she wrapped him up with the blanket and picked him up again, holding him closely against her body.

The baby was cold and stiff, bluish in color, unresponsive and seemingly lifeless. In fact, both parents arrived at the same conclusion, that he was either dead or near death.

By this time, Hae Sun had awakened, pulling herself up on the bars of her crib, she called, "Omma, Omma (Mama, Mama)."

Song picked her up and patted her gently. He said, "Be still my daughter, your little brother may be in big trouble."

They hurriedly dressed and got into the automobile to drive to the doctor's house as quickly as possible. The doctor's office was a bit away in an extension adjoining the doctor's home.

Song knocked at the door to the house and was greeted by the doctor's wife, who was preparing breakfast. On seeing them, she called to the doctor to come quickly.

The doctor led them next door into his office and took the baby from his Mother while Song continued to carry his daughter.

Examining the baby, the doctor noted neither heart nor breath sounds with his stethoscope. Clearly, rigor had begun to set in. There was no sign of injury or disease markers other than the dried mucus in both of the baby's nostrils. Shaking his head sideways, he turned to speak to the baby's parents.

The baby was clearly dead, he told them, most likely dying hours earlier during his sleep. He said sudden deaths occurred in infants and little could be done to prevent or predict their occurrence.

He offered condolences and stood by wringing his hands, wondering if he might have been able to prevent this death with the state of knowledge about infectious diseases he had or with any of the meager stock of medicines available to doctors.

Seeing the Mother sobbing away was a heartbreaking experience the doctor had seen all too often. Song was at a loss as to what to do. The doctor told him he would sign a death certificate and Song would have to file it and arrange for the baby's burial or cremation. He walked with them to the car, saw that the Father was in a suitable state to drive the car, offered them condolences once again, and bid them goodbye.

Song tried to console his wife who began to sob as soon as the doctor had pronounced Hae Jun to be dead, but had little success. She wept unconsolably all the way back to their house, cradling her dead son in her arms. Hae Sun was seated between her and her husband, wondering why her Mother was so distressed and miraculously not crying herself.

They took Hae Jun back to their home where they gently laid him, lifeless, in his own cradle in their bedroom.

Meanwhile, Hae Sun finally began to cry from the accumulated distressfulness of her morning and the nagging, growing tug of hunger.

The cry of the child instantly freed Bok Pil from the depths of sadness she had fallen into and she quickly responded to her living child, setting about to feed her.

Song saw that the mundane matters of life had to go on. And so, he told his wife he would have to make a trip to the shop to obtain money in order to arrange for his son's burial. He promised to hurry back and patted Hae Sun on the head. She was now fully reconstituted back to her sweet self as her hunger pangs dissipated with each mouthful of gruel her Mother offered her.

Song reached the shop when the Colonel who had allowed him to open the concession appeared, seemingly out of nowhere.

He greeted Song, but noticed the gravity in his appearance and inquired of the basis for the gloom. After hearing about the death of his son, the Colonel expressed sincere sorrow and wonder that Song would show up for work on such an occasion.

Song said he had come back to collect money to pay for a proper burial for his son.

On hearing this, the Colonel indicated he was also in charge of other services, only recently becoming the overseer of the base cemetery. He offered Song a burial site, a vault and a proper cement marker for the site. The only thing he could not provide, he said, was a band and a marching color guard.

Unbelievably, Hana-Nim was again at work on his behalf, said Song outloud in Korean to the delight of the Colonel, who did not understand the words, but clearly read their sense as Song broke out in the smile the Colonel had come to expect.

Thus, Song was able to arrange for Hae Jun, a civilian infant, to be buried in the Military Cemetery at Schofield Barracks.

He and his wife had contacted the Reverend Lee to conduct a

grave-side service. A small group of their growing list of friends and the workers and their families gathered for the ceremony.

Standing in the background was the kindly Colonel, who had arranged for the site and a proper marker to be prepared for the burial of Song Suk Soon's and Chun Bok Pil's first born son named Song Hae Jun.

Song saw him and walked over to shake his hand in appreciation of his kindness to them in their time of sorrow. His wife followed a few steps behind holding their daughter Hae Sun.

She bowed down several times and looked up at him to say, "Thank you, very much," in an accented English with her face streaked with tears.

The tall Colonel could hardly hold back his tears as he nodded and reached for Hae Sun's cheeks to softly and gently give them a gentle stroke. "You still have another child, and she is very pretty," he said as he bid them goodbye and turned to leave.

ON WITH LIFE

Song and his wife resumed their lives, immersing themselves in the concession at Schofield and the raising of their daughter, who was given the English name of Evelyn.

He was able to purchase a sewing machine for his wife to use at home and she kept herself even busier by sewing military caps and ties for sale at her husband's shop as well as helping to alter uniforms when the men were swamped with work.

Bok Pil became pregnant again and her husband waited with restrained anxiety for the baby's arrival. The baby was to arrive sometime late in December.

Labor began on Christmas Day, a holiday that he and his family regarded as holy and precious. Before the day had lapsed, the baby was born.

It was a son, larger and heavier than Hae Jun was, dragging the plate of the spring weight to register ten pounds. He cried lustily and could not be consoled until he was placed at his Mother's breast which he searched for and began to suck hungrily even though little came forth. It seemed the sucking was relief enough for this special baby, thought both parents.

Earlier, after a somewhat painful discussion, they had decided to drop reference to Hae or the sea in favor of a name base that was not associated with death. Now, they decided to call their son George in honor of the first President of their new country, Joseph as a middle name after the human Father of Christ, and Sung Tahn as his Korean name which meant a Blessed Event. And so it was that an impressive name, George Joseph Song, was listed on the baby's birth certificate, while he was called Sung Tahn or Tahnney by his parents and sister.

The children grew, Song's business prospered and life continued. The family moved towards Wahiawa into a second story complex on Cane Street to facilitate access to markets and the early education of their daughter. Castner Camp was far from the kindergarten and the elementary school, whereas Cane Street was only a couple of blocks away and in the center of the market area of the little town of Wahiawa.

Two years following Sung Tahn's birth, his wife delivered another son without difficulty. The same Japanese mid-wife supervised the delivery and another handsome baby son was placed in his wife's arms. They named him Sung Gun or Blessed and Diligent, keeping the Sung, still avoiding Hae, and almost anticipating his character by appending Gun to the Sung for diligence.

Sung Gun was smaller than his elder brother, but he was quick in reaching his milestones. As he grew, he often clung to his Mother avoiding the rough necking that frequently engaged his Father and elder brother.

An opportunity to pursue an idea he had been developing over the years arose for Song. Space below their rental unit became available which would be an ideal spot to establish a market with a full meat section. He would stock it with dry and canned goods, some fresh items and a wide variety of butchered products including beef, pork, poultry and fish. He knew the whole sale markets in Honolulu, having worked to pick up and deliver goods for the sugar plantation in the past. His and his wife's experience of going to various small shop dealers around the town for the goods they needed resulted in the expenditure of much too much of their precious time. He believed that housing food items collectively in one store might be a profitable means for housewives with respect to saving time and effort, which could be beneficial to him financially.

He hired a butcher and a sales person and did the wholesale purchasing himself in addition to running the tailor shop. The grocery store fluorished, greatly easing the burden on his wife in the maintenance of her own household and kitchen needs. Now, she merely walked downstairs to shop instead of walking to various parts of town with her babies in tow to collect the necessary materials to fix their meals.

Two years after the birth of his second son, Song's wife was pregnant again. Now space in the living quarters would become an issue.

Song had scoured the town and learned of the leasability of a large piece of property on Lehua Street in the same town of Wahiawa. The piece of property belonged to the Lightfoots who were moving elsewhere. They would lease the property to Song on a yearly basis for a sum not more than what he was paying for the Cane Street complex over the course of a year. The property had not been leased to anyone for some time, as few could afford the year's rental to be paid up front.

It consisted of several acres and had two living quarters, a two-story dwelling for the family and a small detached house for servants. Song reasoned that he could rent out the smaller house and perhaps, rent out part of the acreage for farming to someone, and even have land to spare for raising a few vegetables and animals himself. As his sons grew older, they could help with the work of maintaining a miniature farm, he thought.

Shortly after their move into the Lehua house, his wife delivered the baby, a third son. Unlike her previous babies each of whom was born with very little hair on the head, this one had a head full of black, curly hair. Bok Pil had often spoken of one of her brothers to Song, the pharmacist in Japan, who had curly black hair. Bok Pil herself had wavy strands of hair at the sides. Song was amused to see the wavy tuft of hair on his new son and convinced himself that he would not crop the baby's hair as short as his own. They named him Sung Mahn, or Overwhelmingly Blessed and his sister called him Mahnny.

When the youngest baby was only six months old, Bok Pil was stunned to find herself pregnant again. With four little ones, she already had her hands full. Sung Mahn was only six months old, far too young to have to be weaned before long!

She sought help from her friends who told her of an herbalist who had a means to abort a pregnancy. Several of them had been treated by him before when they had discovered they were pregnant within months of a delivery. Bok Pil visited the herbalist, paid for her herbs, adhered to the instructions she was given and awaited the termination of her pregnancy. Nothing happened for weeks. She returned to the herbalist and was given another package of herbs to take. This regimen was also met by no response. Unable to rid herself of the conceptus, she accepted her fate and endured her confinement.

Delivery was as before with the mid-wife in control and a friend in assistance. The baby was large, weighing in at nine pounds, but was a girl, not another boy as the Mother and her husband had expected. Her head was essentially bald, like her other babies, unlike Sung Mahn. They agreed on Soo Sun or Water Fairy for their second daughter because the Mother had a dream of scooping a baby out of the water, just before the onset of labor.

Now the Mother had five children with the last two just 18 months apart. She had not even begun to wean Sung Mahn when she went into labor with the new baby. While Sung Mahn ate solids, he still nestled in her arms to suckle. He was a beautiful child and his wavy hair had never been cut, but was allowed to grow to shoulder length, prompting many to refer to him as a beautiful girl instead of a boy, despite his masculine dress.

Feeding the newborn had become stressful to Sung Mahn who cried and cried to have his turn at the nipple. The stress of all of these occurrences reduced her milk output making the newborn cry for constant, almost continuous feeding. Finally, Bok Pil decided they might try feeding the newborn with store bought milk. Her husband brought home the canned Carnation Milk which they diluted and offered to the baby. Soo Sun hungrily drank her first bottle of canned milk with such ravenous energy that she was plumb tuckered out at the end and fell soundly asleep. The peacefulness of her sleep after a fully satisfying feeding experience convinced the parents that this was the mode of feeding they would continue with their fifth child.

Meanwhile, Sung Mahn had found the diminutive trickle from his Mother's breast to be fully adequate for his suckling needs and had also fallen asleep. The resulting peace and quiet was just what the parents needed. No further convincing was necessary and a routine was set where the infant was fed with a bottle and

Sung Mahn continued to suckle, ad lib, for more than a year.

About this time, a depression had hit the country, with extenuating effects on the economy of Hawaii. Some workers were being laid off without any promise of rehiring anytime in the near future. People had to eat, so many in the community of Wahiawa came to see Song about purchases of goods at his grocery store on Cane Street, on credit. He allowed them to do so, keeping an account of who bought what in a notebook that was filled by either the butcher or the other hired hand.

By contrast, the tailor shop continued to bring in income as servicemen were not laid off and military decorum was maintained.

Before long however, his own debit ledger for the grocery enterprise had outbalanced the credit side and he was forced to declare bankruptcy. The store and all its effects were sold and all he kept was the ledger filled with notations of unpaid charges made by many town residents, each of whom knew Song well. Song did not seek them out, recognizing that everyone was under duress financially and assured that debtors would eventually repay him, in due course.

Ultimately, only one of the many who owed him was to remember to repay his debt to Song. [In that instance, a gentleman came for a visit unannounced some twenty-five years later, only to be surprised to be invited to lunch. Embarassed, he accepted the kind offer from Song and his wife and after lunch informed them of the nature of his visit. He had come he said, to return the money he owed Song, which had been on his conscience for the past twenty-five years. He thanked them for their patience and their goodness for not seeking repayment from him by legal action.]

Song followed through with the rental of subunits of the large piece of property he had leased. He rented the smaller house for a nominal fee, carved out and rented a large tract for farming and prepared areas for his own family, including a vegetable garden and fenced in plots for chickens, pigs, goats, ducks, and other small animals.

A pig stall was built of concrete where pigs were fed and bred indoors. Everyday, either he or his wife would hose the house down, allowing the water and debris to flow into a canal that had been dug by the town to drain the land around the town during times of heavy rain.

A row of pidgeon nests was also built above the enclosed pig pens and passenger pidgeons were purchased for Song's own amusement. Tags were placed on their legs with his address for notification by acquaintances of their successful delivery of messages. The birds were bred and trained, some successfully and some not, and his two elder sons enjoyed participating in these endeavors.

He also raised a few turkeys and several goats. Sale of the larger animals, the pigs and goats, to others was at a nice profit. He had tried processing one pig on the premises with help from the husband and wife who rented both the smaller house and the farming area, the Haranos, but found the exercise more than he had expected. In particular, storage of the edible pieces was a major challenge. Thereafter, animals were sold to dealers and carted away alive, leaving him free of the burden of sacrificing the animals, let alone the butchering and processing of the carcasses.

Chickens, ducks and turkeys were for his family's own consumption and his wife became adept at handling the entire preparatory process. Eggs were collected daily from the chickens and occasionally from the ducks.

Rabbits were raised to sell to neighbors. No one in his family would allow the rabbits to be sacrificed and served for food and Song had no difficulty finding buyers, especially the family that rented the downstairs quarters of the large house.

At one time, Song even built a number of honey bee hives, perhaps in sentimental tribute to his old friend long since dead, Yong Soo, from whose family his own had bartered for honey. The hives were productive, but keeping the children free of stings became a mission for his wife. The children invariably ran past or into the area and someone or other would invariably become the target of the busy insects with swollen bites to show for these encounters. And so, after a few years of tolerance, Song abandoned these hives and the family purchased their honey, instead.

As he supervised and worked with his wife and young sons to accomplish these activities, he was reminded of his Father's farm in Chongsong. There were stark contrasts, of course, dictated by the difference in climate for one, as well as the availability of many innovative ways to ease labor in Hawaii, for another.

The property had clumps of banana and papaya trees providing fruit for eating all year round. Several tall mango, avocado and other fruit trees provided fruit on a seasonal basis, all coming in the summer months. The yard was bordered by small berry-like red guava bushes as well as another variety bearing fruit about the size of a peach that turned yellow and was both succulent and delicious at the peak of the summer. Vines from the neighboring border separating the property from the land owned by the Water Company extended over and encircled climbing trees, adorning them every summer with luscious passion fruit.

It did not take long before George and his younger siblings discovered these many varieties of edible seasonal fruits on his Father's leased estate. The children waxed and grew in this environment and Song was proud of his family, recording this for posterity in a formal family portrait taken through the aegis of a fellow Korean even as his wife was pregnant with yet another offspring.

SONG'S FAMILY PORTRAIT, 1932

Shortly thereafter, she delivered her seventh baby just three years after the birth of their second daughter. The same mid-wife and friend were there to help. The baby was another girl, their third. She was bald, beautiful and weighed less than eight pounds.

Unbeknowns to the couple, their babies' weights were greater than other oriental babies. The reason was to reveal itself later in life when Bok Pil was discovered with diabetes.

In any event, the birth of their third daughter raised the matter of the selection of a proper name. Jea Sun or the Finest Gift was listed on her birth certificate, but they often referred to her as Kum Ok for Gold and Jade as she was growing up, because they could not choose between the two gems for such a lovely baby.

SONG, HIS WIFE, AND JAE SUN OR JESSIE

Song and his wife saw their family grow, their business at the shop prosper, the fruits of their efforts in the vegetable garden and the backyard animals resulting in the reaping of edible goods and they were glad and happy. Their lives in the community were fulfilling with other families of Korean descent close by, the Korean Christian Church just a block away, an elementary school two blocks away, and the upper grade school only a few miles away.

The depression had affected the community far less than on the continental United States, perhaps because of the absence of large corporations except for the agricultural companies. And there, sugar was a necessary commodity and pineapple, the other crop, was not grown elsewhere in the world to the extent that it was in Hawaii.

Still, times were hard for many as lay-offs occurred and loans were hard to obtain. Because of Song's apparent prosperity during times of hardship for many others in the community, many Koreans came to him for help of one sort or another.

Once a father of a child with a leg cancer who was to have a surgical procedure performed to remove the tumor came by to see him as he was adjusting one of the many posts bracing the wire fence separating the property from the wildly growing intrusive plants on the Water Company's property. He asked for financial help which he could not obtain from the local bank on his credit rating.

Song listened to the man, felt his pain and without much discussion promised to obtain the stated sum for the operation that the doctor had apparently requested before undertaking the task. Song kept his word and obtained the sum from the bank.

How much it was and whether he was ever repaid have never been revealed, not even to his wife, although she had been told about the request. Her response had been for him to help as best as he could and to keep the details to himself, which he apparently did.

Towards the latter part of the depression, political changes around the world began to take ominous forms with aggressive behaviour exhibited both in Europe with Germany taking the lead and in the East involving Japan.

Changes in the military stance of the United States included expansion of facilities in Hawaii, including Schofield Barracks. Consequently, Song was able to expand his operations and was given a second concession. He was even allowed to travel to the site of the military exercises or maneuvers, taking several of his workers to process the khaki and fatigue uniforms of the men for the several weeks of training they spent away from the base. On these occasions, Song commuted to the fields returning in time to drive his wife and the other workers who remained at the shop back home.

Bok Pil had by this time begun to puff on Bull Durham cigarettes which she rolled herself. One or two a day was about all she allowed herself, but it was something she enjoyed doing in her husband's presence when he was also smoking a Chesterfield.

After their marriage in 1919, Bok Pil had received news from Korea that her eldest brother, his family and her Mother were moving to Yokohama, Japan. Apparently, her eldest brother found a means to use his knowledge of Japanese and Korean to better financial advantage to support his increasing obligations. Periodically, letters would arrive from Japan to keep her informed of the status of the family. Eventually, even her sister and her family moved to Yokohama, completing the Chun family circle except for herself. A family portrait reflecting her absence was sent to her. She had this photograph mounted in a frame and hung in the living room at Lehua Street.

CHUN FAMILY IN YOKOHAMA, JAPAN

In 1935, Bok Pil received news of the serious illnesses of both her Mother, who was apparently dying and her second brother, the pharmacist, who was suffering from renal failure.

Suk Soon agreed to her traveling to Yokohama, Japan to visit her dying Mother and seriously ill brother. She decided to take her youngest daughter along to relieve the load on Hae Sun or Evelyn, who would be responsible for managing the household in her absence.

She set sail on a liner with gifts for everyone in her family in Yokohama. Looking out over the railing again for the first time since her departure from Korea sixteen years before, brought back sad memories.

Here she was, looking across the way to a family filled with anxiety at her departure, while she was also carrying her own anxious burdens, wondering if she would arrive in time to see her Mother. She wondered about the condition and eventual welfare of her brother with the renal disease, her reception and reaction to the nation that had subjugated Koreans to a menial status, and the mundacity of the voyage inconveniences itself, particularly as it might affect her youngest daughter, who was not even three years of age.

It took a whole week to reach Japan. They arrived in Tokyo where she was met by her eldest brother and her elder sister.

They greeted each other with tears, awaiting the question foremost in Bok Pil's mind, "How is Omoni (Mother)?"

Her eldest brother told her that she had died, apparently on the very day of her departure from Hawaii and that she had been cremated and buried, as was the custom in Japan.

Bok Pil broke out in tears and wails, alarming her young daughter, who began to cry. She tried to compose herself as best she could, explaining to Jea Sun that everything was alright. The child continued to cry still alarmed and panicked by the newness of everyone and everything. The only way she could be consoled was by her Mother holding her close to her chest, gently patting her on the back, uttering soothing words.

After the child began to calm down, they boarded a bus to Yokohama where a number of Koreans lived in homes around a small market area sporting goods in Korean. This was the earliest "Korea Town" in Yokohama where immigrant Koreans resided in Japan as noncitizens. Japanese citizenship was not available to them and would remain the case despite the birth of a second and even a third generation of Koreans in Japan.

Bok Pil and her daughter were greeted by the rest of the Chun family including her very sick brother. Expressions of joy and sorrow all mixed together and were shared in the atmosphere of the several homes in which they gathered.

A visit to the cemetary was made where Bok Pil was startled at the size of the plot containing her Mother's remains. It was a square measuring about nine inches, similar to others at this site. Ashes are placed in ceramic vases for burial, which do not take much space, she was told.

Her brother had a sallowness of his skin, swollen feet and legs and seemed to be totally without energy. He visited the hospital every several days and was on a rigid diet of some sort that excluded most of the pickled and spicy Korean dishes. He was wan, but remained handsome with curly hair and had a modestly groomed moustache above his upper lip.

His sister's young daughter enthralled him and he laughed with genuine pleasure at her jabbering about this and that in English and Korean, seemingly unhindered by language barriers, moving from one to the other with great facility.

After a stay of nearly a month, Bok Pil and her daughter returned to Hawaii, leaving a dying brother and the rest of the Chun family in Japan, including the remains of her dear Mother all reduced to a handful of ashes in a Japanese cemetary. Crossing Tae-pyung-yang again, Bok Pil spent much time on deck facing the east, towards Hawaii, leaving Asia far behind, forever.

Soon after, Bok Pil developed symptoms of hyperthyroidism. With a goiter to be found on palpation and her eyes showing the classical rim of white above the pupils, the doctor made the diagnosis and removed the goiter surgically. During her recovery, she began to exhibit symptoms of diabetes mellitus. These disturbances not withstanding, she continued her hard work, helping her husband with his business, caring for the household and her children and expending much emotional energy keeping in touch with her family in Yokohama.

Her second brother eventually died of renal failure leaving her to grieve alone, thousands of miles away from her family. Because of a persistent "thumping of her heart", her physician advised her to stop smoking entirely, which she did.

Thus, Bok Pil had to adjust her dietary intake, check her urinary glucose output on a daily basis and carefully adjust the dose of insulin which she injected into her thigh every morning. She learned how to do this extremely well and had only one bout of ketoacidosis many years after the diagnosis of insulin-dependent diabetes mellitus had been made. Quite on her own, she resorted to pounding water cress in an old coffee can with a mallet, squeezing the juice and drinking the juice from a large bunch almost daily. In addition, she made it a point to eat a whole tomato almost every day.

Amazingly, years later the benefits of antioxidants in various disease states have slowly acrued. Intuitively, Bok Pil served herself well and survived more than thirty years after the diagnosis of diabetes mellitus was made on her with very few complications.

Song had no apparent physical problems, but one evening after retiring rather early, he had a generalized seizure, which was caught by his wife. He bit his tongue, which bled, of course, and he thrashed about for a few moments, foaming at the mouth. The physician was called in and Song was injected with phenobarbital. Workup did not reveal a localizing focus. He spoke of an injury to the head as a young man, which had left a scar on his scalp. Apparently, the incident was without serious immediate consequences. Considering all things, the doctor placed him on phenobarbital for over a year before withdrawal. He advised him to stop drinking alcohol and to stop smoking. Song never touched another drop of alcohol or smoked another cigarette thereafter and remained free of seizures.

KOREAN COMMUNITY LIFE AND SOLIDARITY

RELIGIOUS LIFE

Each of the children had been baptised at the Korean Christian Church. Each attended Sunday services at the same church, earlier for Sunday School and staying on for services held in Korean when they were older.

Song's wife attended regularly, dressed in Korean dress at first but later donning western styled clothes she made herself.

Song did not attend services on a regular basis. Every week, he made sure his children and wife attended whereas he was more likely to remain at home to complete a chore or two. While he worked, he prayed to Hana-nim in the privacy of each endeavor. He prayed for good health, safety for everyone, continued prosperity, and for forgiveness of all their sins, including his.

CHRISTMAS CELEBRATIONS

At Christmas, elaborate preparations were made at Church to present a pageant of the birth of Christ. Song attended every one of these.

A chorus of adult and children singers set the background music, lights were dimmed or lit for the shepherds in the fields watching their flocks by night, angels were dressed with halos and wings to announce the miraculous birth, elaborately dressed Kings walked single file down the aisle carrying their gold, frankincense and myrrh, and all knelt before a cradle with the swaddled doll representing Jesus beside a kneeling Mary all draped with a shawl and Joseph standing tall beside her holding a staff.

The singing of "Joy to the World the Lord is Come" marked the end of the pageant after which Santa Claus walked in from the door laughing, "Ho, ho, ho, Merry Christmas!"

Small boxes of candy were distributed to everyone to end the program.

Then, amidst a clamor of good wishes, the congregation slowly left for home, including the performers who quickly changed back into their street clothes without bothering to wipe the makeup off their faces.

Back at home, it was not until some years later that an artificial Christmas tree was purchased together with decorative pieces for display before repacking and storage for reuse in ensuing years.

EASTER CELEBRATIONS

At Easter following Sunday School where the meaning of Easter was reviewed and rejoyced, the children hunted for real boiled and colored eggs that had been hidden in the Church yard. After the hunt was over, the one with the largest find won a prize-usually a stuffed rabbit. Everyone was given a small straw basket filled with artificial grass and various sweets, and of course, all of the eggs they found.

The custom of searching for eggs was extended at home by the Mother who learned to dye eggs a lovely brown using the dry outside peels of round onions. She would hide the eggs about in the large property, keeping the limits within the area beyond the veranda. Her children scoured the area, peeking under brushes and plants to discover large oval shaped brown magic here and there and even nestled in the joints of branching tree limbs.

These two special days, Christmas and Easter, were celebrated in pretty much the same format each year. Good Friday was also important and was observed with a quiet service early in the evening without fanfare and largely without children in attendance.

NEW YEARS CELEBRATION

New Years day was another special holiday, but it was the eve that stood out in every child's mind. Preparations were elaborate including the washing of all clothing and bedding, the scrubbing of the house from top to bottom and discarding left over foods except for the pickled goods. Everyone had to take a bath and wash his hair. Nails had to be clipped before midnight. Thus, all of the old was discarded, trimmed, or washed away to make way for the new.

Culinary traditions were also expressed with the preparation of special dishes including tok (rice-cake) and mundoo (beef and pickled vegetable dumpling) served in chicken broth together with choen (fried seasoned beef or chicken dipped in an egg batter) and an array of vegetable dishes. Varieties of sweetened tok were also available. Everyone had a small bite of other foods to eat around dinner time, but the special feast was not eaten until after the stroke of midnight had been heard.

Midnight was announced by the blasting of fireworks throughout the community. Firecrackers blasted in single bursts or in a sequence of bursts when individual or clusters of firecrackers were lit with a lighted "punk", a thin metal or wooden rod coated with an organic substance that stayed smoldering after being lit. Firecrackers ranged in size from "baby" ones about 3/4 of an inch in length and several millimeters in diameter to multiples of these, all the way to large ones that were never allowed to be used by Song's children, at least not in his presence. Metal rods coated with fireworks that did not explode called "stars" were lighted and twirled in the dark. Rocket flares were also shot up into the air to break out into a shower of light.

After the fireworks were all discharged, the family gathered for their first meal of the New Year and everyone wished each other a happy year. Not too infrequently, the younger ones leaned back in their chairs half-asleep after taking only a few bites of the delicious meal. However, there would always be enough to offer the next day, New Year's Day.

LANGUAGE SCHOOL

Each child attended Korean Language School after regular classes in school. Classes were held at the Korean Christian Church located a block away from Song's home on Lehua Street and lasted for two hours after regular school. Children were separated by grade, mixed by gender and were taught to read hangul, the phonetic language using textbooks supplied to each child.

These classes kept the children busy after school, taught them their parents' language, perpetuated knowledge of the culture from which their parents came, and allowed them to interact and bond with one another.

At the end of each school year, exercises were held when prizes were given and a program was presented for which the children had prepared to perform special Korean dances and songs. Thus, the folk songs and dances of Korea became familiar to the second generation of Koreans raised near the Korean Christian Church in Wahiawa around the period in which Song and his wife were raising their family.

ANNUAL CHURCH PICNIC

Once a year, the Church members flocked together at the beach in Haleiwa on a Sunday sometime in the summer. A brief service was held followed by the engagement of the congregation in group competitions like volleyball and relay races. Families brought their own picnic fare, spreading blankets out for their use. Families visited with each other, swam in the ocean, and searched for crabs, snails and shells along the lava rocks that stood at both ends of the bay of waters along the sandy beach at Haleiwa.

Everyone returned with a sunburn, back to Wahiawa, located in the middle of the island of Oahu, surrounded by pineapple fields, located between two lakes of a single reservoir, near Schofield Barracks and Wheeler Field.

MARCH THE FIRST, OR SAMIL

The first day of March was always a time of special gathering to celebrate Samil. This special event, the Samil-undong (the third month's first day celebration), commemorated the date when Koreans in Seoul rallied and demonstrated for independence from the Japanese on March 1, 1919. A proclamation for independence was issued, signed by 33 prominent Koreans, and supported by a peaceful march of Koreans.

The Japanese killed over 500 demonstrators, wounded over twice that number and imprisoned more than 19,000 others. It would mark a dark day in Korean history and would be remembered with sorrow by Koreans everywhere with a call for freedom and restitution of Korea's sovereignty.

The Korean flag and the American flag were both displayed at these gatherings, prayers were said, political matters were discussed and everyone stood up singing the Korean national anthem followed by shouts of "Dong-nip Mansei, Mansei (independence or freedom for 10,000 years)!" Feelings of linkage with the home of their parents and ancestors arose in each of the children as they regularly participated in these ceremonies.

Sometimes their pro-Korean feelings aroused anti-Japanese sentiments, interferring with their interactions with Japanese classmates. Invariably, the best friends of the children tended to be either Korean or of a different ethnic group when they were young. Of course, as they grew older, friendships no longer excluded people of Japanese ancestry. In fact, strong relationships were forged between Song's children and some of their Japanese friends, several of which were to extend for years and years to come.

SUMMER TIME ACTIVITIES AND WILD LIFE

Summers presented the children with time to explore the woods in the property of the Wahiawa Water Company. This property spanned a distance to a small lake where the cleverest fish in the world lived, escaping with the bait nearly every time. Only an occasional one was caught by any one of the boys and then their Mother was not sure whether the creature was edible. Of course, fishing was forbidden, but the boys rigged their own poles and managed to acquire hooks and bait for these excursions.

The property offered a myriad of "wildlife" experiences. Mongooses imported to control the rats in the agricultural fields of Hawaii fluorished, soon overpopulating the lush terrain that supported the rat population. Exploits into the wild, initially armed with slingshots, then with BB guns, offered the boys an exciting opportunity to seek and "destroy" the enemy. Some of these beasts would bare their fangs and charge, adding to the excitement of their adventures. There were plenty of trees to scale in the event of a "charge", but these slender, lithe creatures were more apt to run past you to the other side and away, than to attack.

Doves abounded and were fair game to Song's son for they were delicious when broiled over charcoal. The abundance of these had not raised the issue of conservation at that time in Hawaii.

Wild pigs were said to be around the area, too, but none was ever encountered in the property adjoining the Song's leasehold.

CHILDRENS' PORTRAITS BEFORE WWII

Hae Sun was called Evelyn in English. She had managed the cooking and cleaning while her Mother was away in Japan in 1935, a formidable task for a girl of fifteen.

As a young teenager, she had developed a taste for Korean pop-songs, enjoying the lyrics as well as the melodies on the series of ceramic discs she urged her parents to acquire. Naturally, some of the singers were handsome young men whose pictures were displayed on the brochures that arrived with the records and Evelyn developed a "crush" on one or two, like any teenager.

Evelyn wanted to play the piano, but Song could not afford such an instrument at that time. Instead, he painted the scales on a piece of wood to the near dimensions of the piano at Church for Evelyn to "practice", which she did for many years. An occasional foray to the Church when it was not in session did help, somewhat, but could not sustain her interest in the piano.

By 1941, Evelyn had graduated from high school and departed for college in Los Angeles, California. She had been a devoutly religous young lady, who spent many hours reading the scriptures from cover to cover.

When asked why she had not finished reading the book, she would reply, "Oh, I did finish reading it several times already, but I have to reread it not once more, but over and over again to better understand what it says."

She sailed away on the ocean liner, Matsonia, decked out with floral necklaces or leis given to her by her family and a group of girlfriends who came to bid her "aloha". She enrolled and completed her college education at the Bible Institute of Los Angeles or BIOLA, receiving her degree after the Japanese sneak attack on Pearl Harbor.

George had grown handsome and tall. He was athletically talented and went out for pole vaulting, track, and jumping the hurdles. His father followed his physical exploits with a great deal of interest. In fact, he purchased a series of increasingly heavier and longer bamboo poles for training at home, had a special pole vaulting site prepared on the leased property, built a number of hurdle bariccades for use, prepared a baseball field for George, his younger brothers and the neighborhood boys to play in, and purchased a series of increasingly larger bicycles for his use.

After graduation from high school, George attended the University of Hawaii and was a member of their Reserved Officers Training Corps or ROTC. The University was in Honolulu and George commuted in a second car that Song purchased for this purpose.

George could play the ukelele extremely well and was often found strumming or picking at the instrument and humming along. Drawing and painting also proved to be skills that he had as judged by the several amazingly beautiful pieces he had created with pencil, charcoal, and even water color and brush.

The pressures of college and the commuting offered little time to continue these pursuits after graduation from high school.

George majored in premedicine with every intent on becoming a doctor, but for the timing of the attack on Pearl Harbor. But, more of this later.

Sung Gun was given the English name of Henry. He was also an excellent student and had a remarkable talent for music. He took up the violin in junior high school and rapidly developed the ability to produce beautiful and eloquent sounds. He was featured as a soloist at numerous school events and was urged to try for a place with the Honolulu Symphony Orchestra by his high school music teacher, Miss Brown. He was selected to play in the Orchestra and continued to delight his family with the increasingly wider and more profound pieces that he rehearsed over and over in the evenings to reach perfection.

Despite his smaller size, he was not to be outdone in athletics. He went out for high school football and would be remembered for his outstanding catch of the kickoff ball, running all the way across the field to a touchdown. He also tried baseball with the boys who gathered around the field in their yard. With his short legs, he nimbly and hurriedly ran this way or that, all the while keeping an eye on the ball to catch nearly every ball coming within his sector in the outfield. He was also an excellent tennis player and played hand-ball extremely well.

Bicycling was something else he executed well, frequently showing off his ability to cycle without holding the bars, much to the admiration of his siblings, and the anxiety of his parents.

He quickly learned to roller skate at the rink located only a few blocks away from their Lehua Street home. Soon he was able to spin and twirl quite gracefully and could race around the rink faster than almost anyone else.

In December of 1941, he was a student at Leilehua High School, just next to Schofield Barracks.

Sung Mahn was named Andrew in English. He was a gregarious, lively fellow seemingly never alone, but nearly always in the midst of a gaggle of buddies. His affable style and good nature won him many friends and no identifiable enemies.

He had a hobby of making model airplanes and ships of every sort out of balsalm wood which he would carefully glue together, then dress with tissue paper which he sprinkled with water to tighten the fit just right before meticulously painting and decorating them to reproduce a miniature ship or plane of some renown.

Andy or Mahnny as he was called also had a penchant for music. In Junior High School, he took up the clarinet and before long was tooting as well as anyone playing songs the family heard on the radio which had been introduced to the family at the request of Evelyn. He readily moved from the clarinet to the saxophone, playing one instrument or the other with great ease and facility. In addition, Mahnny had a beautiful tenor voice and could often be heard singing sad English ballads like Danny Boy.

He dabbled in all of the sports his older brothers engaged in, but found another, younger crowd of boys with whom he mostly played the same sports. He was creative in sports, learning to slide barefooted in mud puddles after a rain shower, skidding back and forth without a fall. He even introduced his younger sibling Soo Sun to this activity.

Of course, with his wavy hair and personality, no one had enough digits to number the girls who bore "crushes" on him. He had just begun high school when war broke out.

Soo Sun, or Ellen, was in the seventh grade at the start of the war. She had grown unusually tall for an Asian, towering over many of her classmates, both boys and girls.

She had a penchant for climbing trees around the yard-especially one avocado tree with an outstretched limb. She was frequently to be found there by her older sister who had the aggravating task of cajoling her to descend "forthwith" for her nightly bath before supper. A non-edible berry tree arching over the fence separating the yard from the Water Company property was also a favorite of hers not only for the passion fruit that could be found in the summer, but for the height to which one could climb to almost reach God, she thought.

Many years later, she came to recognize the influence her older sister's devotion to God had made on her. In her own way, she was also constantly seeking the face of God in every encounter in her life.

She tried the violin and after nearly a full school year, the music teacher asked her to switch to the cello. Several reasons were given for this: no one had selected the cello and the orchestra needed a cellist; there was an overabundance of violin players; a taller student would be better to play the instrument and she was the tallest and might learn to play the cello quickly because she was, after all, Henry Song's sister. After a year on the cello, she dropped music entirely because of the frustration of having to catch up with the other sections and the nuisance of carting the large instrument to and from school.

Instead, she had decided on her own to study the piano, despite the lack of one in their home. She registered for Class Piano and arranged to practice piano on her own through the local Korean Christian Church, an arrangement she personally made with the minister. She was allowed to use the piano for practice on Saturdays.

Soo Sun was in the first half of the seventh grade in

December of 1941.

Jea Sun was named Jessie, but everyone called her Oggie. She was a dainty and gracious young lady, learning to cope with five older siblings by smiling and not raising a fuss.

Just around the age of three, she was the only one to accompany her Mother on her sad voyage by steamship to visit her family residing in Yokohama, Japan.

Somewhere in her early life she acquired the neatest set of freckles that lightly peppered both cheeks but left the bridge of her nose free. Her dimples not withstanding, she was also very feminine.

Oggie could draw and paint beautifully, first using crayons or pencil and paper, then moving to charcoal, and water color. Eventually, she learned how to paint using oil and canvass and completed several outstanding pieces.

Oggie loved dolls and stuffed animals. Shirley Temple caught the attention and hearts of the young children in those days and Oggie was no exception. To celebrate one Christmas, Oggie received a beautiful replica of the actress as a large doll with eyes that closed, arms and legs that could be moved, and a curly top of brownish-yellow hair. In addition, she received a Teddy Bear that stood as tall as the doll. Her delight over these gifts brought everyone to Ooh and Aah in counterpoint. These toys participated in make-believe dramas and were over fed with play china and bottles. They and other toys brought her much joy as she grew and matured.

Oggie also had the voice of a nightingale, often breaking into a sweet soprano warble, enlightening the family. Thus, she did not have to learn to play a man made instrument, instead relying on her own God-given vocal cords to generate beautiful sounds.

She had just entered the fourth grade at the outbreak of the war.

DECEMBER 7, 1941

In December of 1941, Evelyn was in Los Angeles, finishing up with her studies at BIOLA. Earlier, she had written about a friendly family, the Lee's, who had invited her over for dinner and lunch on a number of occasions. Later, she revealed that their youngest son, Warren Hardy Lee, was in college and was changing his major to theology, planning a move to Chicago to attend the Moody Bible Institute. It became clear that a romantic attachment had developed between Evelyn and Hardy as Lee was called, and the Songs looked forward to its fully blooming.

Sometime in the fall of 1941, George had returned home from a brief journey to see if he could transfer to the University of California. He was in a transition period and spent time working in the yard and at his Father's shop. During this time, he built a platform in a berry tree near the house where he spent some time away from the hubub of life with younger siblings and frequently could be heard strumming his ukelele and singing.

The house was a two story one with a large bank of stairs leading to the top floor where the family lived. It opened to a screened veranda where the family ate their meals. The kitchen was set immediately beside the veranda as did the living room just adjoining the kitchen. From the veranda, one could see four doors, three of which opened to bedrooms and the fourth, next to the kitchen, opened into a long narrow hall leading to the bathroom.

Everyone was asleep on Sunday morning, the 7th of December in 1941. It was customary for Soo Sun to collect the morning paper, the Advertiser, which was left on the lower steps by the carrier who traveled by bicycle. Soon after dawn had broken, Soo Sun rose, spent a few moments in the bathroom, and prepared to retrieve the Sunday newspaper.

A droning of planes could be heard, unusual for Sunday, she thought to herself. Wheeler Field, the army airfield located next to Schofield Barracks was where the planes would have originated from, and so she was used to the sounds of planes as they took off or landed. But not on Sunday mornings.

She also heard something else--a repetitive distant thud, thud, thud, like muffled explosions. Furthermore, the roaring sounds of planes alternately changed now and then, as though the planes were diving or/and climbing.

As she drew back the curtains surrounding the screens of the veranda, she scanned the horizon as customary and looked off in the direction of Wheeler Field. She was surprised to see a column of black smoke rising high above the level of the surrounding trees, something she had never seen before.

Unhooking the latch to the front door, she stepped out and down the stairs for the paper. Just above their front yard, she noticed several planes passing along, revving their engines, apparently chasing each other. In fact, they seemed to be firing on each other in mock attack, because she heard what sounded like fireworks popping about.

She hurried back up the stairs and went straight to her Mother's room. Mother was just rising out of bed, ready to begin her long, never-ending, daily work.

"Omoni, how come there are a lot of airplanes today? I also hear them making strange sounds like they were shooting at each other. Are they on maneuvers, do you think?" Soo Sun asked as she planted her daily kiss on her Mother's cheek.

Her Mother responded that she had not heard of the artillery going on such activity, but then the airforce was a different matter, not like the Army which informed all essential concessions in a timely fashion to prepare for maneuvers.

With that, she stretched and trotted off to clean up, dress, and start preparing breakfast, the first of a long list of duties she would do for her family before the day would end.

One by one, the rest of the family got up and gathered to eat breakfast at the table set on the veranda. From here on a clear day, as this was, one could see the backyard clear to the stunning view of the mountain ranges far away coming to a V-like joint to form Kolekole Pass.

This morning, spots could be seen moving through the pass-- an unusual sight at any time, and even more so for the spots were airplanes and the day was Sunday.

The black column of smoke rising over Wheeler Field to the left was also noted by others of the family. There was a strange background thud, thud, thud and variable sounds of planes either gaining speed or decelerating. Everyone soon developed an uneasy sense that something strange was going on. Not long after, the sound of planes flying at variable speeds over their yard returned again.

Mahnny detected the rising sun decorating the wings of one of them, recognizing the plane as a Japanese Zero. He shouted this out and ran out to the railing of the steps to free himself from the bothersome cross hairs of the wire netting encircling the veranda.

"Yeah, it's a Japanese Zero and it's fighting with the American plane, a P-40!" he shouted with great excitement.

The notion that this was a deliberate attempt by Americans to simulate the possible enemy in an airborne exercise was raised as a likely scenario. No news of any disturbance was heard on the radio. Everything else seemed to be proceeding as usual. Yet, there was this peculiar, unsettling feeling shared by all. The droning of the planes, the bursts of rat-atat-atats, and the distant thudding spelled something extraordinary was occurring. These were not the usual sounds heard when maneuvers were underway.

Before long, the wail of a firetruck could be heard. The boys dashed off to investigate. Soon they were back with news that the local elementary school located only a couple of blocks away was on fire. The circumstance for the blaze was not entirely clear to anyone.

It was not until afternoon that the radio announcer broke in with the following news, "We interrupt this program to announce that the island of Oahu has been attacked by airplanes of the Empire of Japan."

The news stunned everyone striking fear because they had all known of the brutality of the Japanese in Korea and in China. Moreover, most of the immediate community consisted of Japanese immigrants--what would they do in the event of an invasion, which surely would follow?

The radio announced that a blackout and curfew had been mandated and everyone was to obey. The National Guard was activated and all able-bodied men, even Boy Scouts, were asked to present themselves at the local police station to help out in the emergency situation.

George had been a member of the ROTC at the University of Hawaii and each of the boys had been active as Boy Scouts. So, all three reported to the local police station to lend their assistance with Song's approval, but Song himself remained at home. Each was placed on patrol duty to enforce the curfew and daily the boys were away for various durations of time.

Meanwhile, Song and his wife took strips of dark cloth and taped their windows. Song also rushed out to the markets to fill the larder with staples and fill the cars with gas. He parked the cars away from the house and moved combustible cleaning materials away into the field, under trees. Just in case of a water shortage, jugs of water were collected.

Soo Sun found herself shaking with fright, visualizing a fiery onslought on her home and loved ones. She followed her Father closely, helping him with the various preparations to minimize their exposure to danger. Noticing her shivers and frightened look, Father reassured her that the United States Army could not be beaten and would thwart any invasion by the Japanese.

It was late when the boys returned the first day. They talked about the fire at the elementary school noting that there were no reported casualties. However, they did witness a neighboring Korean family rushing around carrying one of their daughters who was about a year older than Soo Sun. She had been hit in the groin by a shrapnel during a dog fight between a Japanese Zero and an American P40. Fortunately, she was not critically injured but had to be rushed to the doctor's office for a successful surgical removal of the bullet.

The boys had also seen the bodies of several badly burned Japanese pilots retrieved from planes that had crashed in the pineapple fields nearby. They described the scene and the scent of the burnt enemy pilot bodies lying on the floor at the local fire station. The gruesomeness of the details made the rest of the family recoil and tune out.

News of similar sort filled the airwaves as the remainder of the family sat huddled around the radio the next day. Everyone was advised to stay at home except for the Civilian Patrol.

The boys were out on patrol again, presumably looking for the possibility of strange behaviour on the part of the Japanese populace. As it turned out, no such activity was to be found. In fact, the Japanese immigrants and their children were just as frightened as we were about the marauding attackers and were cooperating as best as possible to maintain civil obedience and to curtail extraneous activities that might hamper the military or local government authorities.

Everyone experienced a heightened sense of anxiety and tension during the early days after the Japanese attack. Their entire pattern of living had been altered with the boys away for long periods of time and both parents staying at home, appearing anxious and worried. Their usual interactions were altered and after dusk, everyone had to be indoors except for the guards and troops. At bedtime, everyone had difficulty falling asleep until late into the wee hours of the early morning.

On December 10th, three days after the attack on Pearl Harbor, George took a taxi from Wahiawa to Honolulu instead of driving his car to serve as a volunteer with the Home Guard. He had not informed his parents, but felt frustrated without arms to protect himself, his family or his community. The driver happened to be a Japanese man, inciting some anxiety on George's part, but he quickly sensed the driver was as unnerved as he was about the Japanese sneak attack.

At the Armory in Honolulu, he was formally inducted and was subsequently issued uniforms and a rifle with bullets. A few days later, he was sent to his base camp in Wahiawa, a Civilian Construction Corps (CCC) camp used to house federal construction workers. There, he finally had access to a telephone and called his parents, explaining what had transpired and where he had been assigned.

George's failure to return after his departure to "go on duty" on the 10th of December had left his parents in deep consternation. They worried about the possibility of his induction into a fighting unit, but could not locate him. They had frantically made the usual inquiries with the police and the guard headquarters, to no avail.

Hearing from him, they quickly gathered necessary clothing and other items and visited him at the CCC camp. The meeting was full of emotional outbursting on the part of the Mother, as might be expected. Just knowing where he was brought comfort to them however and, thereafter, they went by periodically with various goods they knew he would not reject.

George's unit, the 298th Infantry from Oahu, marched to Kahuku, a distance away, where they readied a defensive position, digging trenches, storing ammunition, practicing and posting guard.

All normal work activities were suspended the first several days after the sneak attack on Hawaii. Curfew was mandated, blackouts continued, and before long shelves at the local grocery sites became barer and barer.

With the lifting of the curfew, Song returned to the shop to find new regulations and restrictions had been imposed. Gasoline was rationed requiring everyone with a car to register for receipt of tickets for gas. Whereas his wife helped him at the shops more regularly now that the children were older and did not require constant supervision, her help became vital as workers soon began to move, one by one, to higher paying defense-linked labor that sprung up all over the island, especially at Pearl Harbor.

School was suspended for weeks during which alternative sites had to be identified for Leilehua High School. Leilehua High School, located immediately adjacent to Schofield Barracks, was taken over by the military leaving the community with a desperate need to find sites of sufficient size and accessibility for use as a temporary school.

The immediate solution for the community was to confiscate a large Japanese Language School that had operated in the town of Wahiawa. Together with several other community or church related sites, a sufficient number of classrooms was identified for use to continue the high school courses. These practices continued until a new Leilehua High School was constructed, in due course, located towards the hills diametrically opposite to the old site outside of Schofield Barracks.

Song and his wife followed these developments closely, making sure their younger ones were enrolled on time for continuation of their education. Through his own initiative but with full support from his parents, Henry completed high school education at Mid-Pacific Institute, a private boarding school in Honolulu.

There were many other changes in their lives. For example, eeveryone was issued a gas mask which had to be carried everywhere. The issuance came with live instructions of how and when to use these potentially life-saving devices. While they were comforted knowing they had the means to survive a gas attack, the idea of a need for these devices unnerved most islanders.

Bomb shelters had to be dug for each household and these were inspected by civilian teams. Each shelter was to be stocked with a flashlight and non-perishable foods and water to last a few days. Mock air raid practices were held with the sirens at the local fire stations blaring and then wailing loudly and incessantly after which all citizens were held to a protocol of turning off all lights in their houses and cars, jumping into bomb raid shelters, and remaining still until the all-clear signal was sounded. Song and his sons and the Haranos, their Japanese tenant neighbors, dug a common shelter to share along with their stock should a real need arise.

Fresh fruits and vegetables from the west coast of the United States soon disappeared from the market. Beef and pork products were hard to find. The family learned to depend on the products of their own mini-farm for eggs, chicken and duck as meat products, vegetables from their own garden or purchased from Mr. Harano, their tenant and farmer, and the fruits that abounded in their yard.

The rationing of gasoline severely limited Song's ability to freely conduct the operations of his trade. Everyone with a car was issued so many tickets for a set volume of gasoline, irrespective of his need for all of it, or not. Once, in a pinch for more gas, Song paid someone for his allotted ration book and refilled his car using one of the issued tickets. This manner of acquiring more gasoline for use was a common practice in the community. Soon after paying for the gas at the station, he was arrested by a local policeman who was on the lookout for "illegal ration book users" and summarily locked in the local jail.

Failing to return home before dark, his family searched frantically for him without success. Finally, they reported his missing status to the police where to their surprise, they learned of his incarceration. The charge was his illegal use of someone else's ration allotment. The fact of his payment for the book not withstanding, he was so charged and had to spend the night in jail.

Finally back at home in the morning, he warned each and everyone of his children to never, never shortcut the law, even if it appeared legitimate, as he thought his action had been. We were never to circumvent the law, no matter what, he warned.

"The law is the law," he said.

Thereafter, he found other means to accomplish his tasks, mostly postponing trips until absolutely necessary.

The greatest concern pressing the family had to do with whether or not George would be shipped off to the front. Initially, George was commissioned a Corporal but soon rose to Sargeant and then became a Staff Sargeant in his unit. The 298th Infantry occupied Tent City in the hills surrounding the area of Kahuku before moving in to wooden barracks.

Two years later, the 298th Infantry was incorporated into the 24th Division and was shipped out across the Pacific to Guadalcanal.

His family was unaware of his destination although they were informed of an imminent move to come. Months later, word came to the family designating a special APO or Army Post Office address for correspondence to be received by George. No disclosure was made of his location throughout this period. Letters to cheer him and packages were dispatched through this address on a regular basis. His family hung on every word in his letters and his Mother kept every one. All the while, no one had any idea where George was except that he was somewhere on some island in the Pacific Ocean or Tae-pyung-yang.

Meanwhile, during the summer before he was to graduate from Mid-Pacific High School, Henry worked as a carpenter/painter at Wheeler Field. He described having to scrape off dried blood from the walls of the hangers at the Field before repairing and repainting the structures. The blood had been left by the injured and dying on the 7th of December.

Following graduation from high school, Henry was drafted into the army. After a brief period of orientation, he was shipped to the continental US for further training.

Now, Song's wife hung a flag with two stars in her bedroom window signifying the dedication of two of her sons towards the effort to keep her adopted country free.

Henry was stationed on the continental United States serving in the army in some intelligence area. News from him centered around his health and the weather with little about the work he was engaged in. His APO address changed from time to time lending the family a view of his movement from area to region on the continent of the United States. But, that was all. No word of the actual work he was doing nor of the cities nearby was ever revealed.

Reports of the progress of the war were followed closely by Song who had his younger children, either Mahnny or Soo Sun, to read excerpts of the two newspapers they subscribed, the evening Star Bulletin and the morning Advertiser. The events and turns of each battle were closely followed such that the names of previously unheard of places and persons became household words--for Song and his wife were deeply involved with their two sons serving in the U.S. Army.

His wife could hardly be consoled when news of fighting in the South Pacific turned sour. She was sure one or both of her sons might be involved, although she would not know exactly where or in what capacity either might have been involved until years later.

Song's 60th birthday came and went in 1943 without the celebration traditionally held in old Korea. Life span was shorter in those days and a parent reaching 60 was special and an occasion for great jubilation in Korea. Song's 60th birthday arrived in the middle of the war when victory for the U.S. was not assured, a time when half of his offsprings were away from home, two in the military and the third married to a student in Chicago. Also, it was a time when he was stressed at work without sufficient craftsmen and laborers to help because they had moved to defense-related activities for higher salaries. Furthermore, gas rationing was in place, food items were limited in availability, especially beef and pork products, making a large celebration virtually unthinkable.

As it turned out, following a ten month tour of duty in the jungles of Guadalcanal, George was selected to attend Officers Cadidate School (OCS) in the U.S. Two weeks of furlough brought him home to Lehua Street and the happiest family in the whole neighborhood! The whites of his eyes were stained yellow in reaction to the anti-malarial medication he had to take to prevent malaria. He looked more mature and seemed wiser. During this furlough, he met his future wife, Soo Nam Chung, a lovely young lady from Honolulu. She was about to embark for college in Vermont. Their relationship blossomed and flourished while both were on the continental U.S.A., George at OCS and Soo Nam in college.

Just prior to the end of the war with the Japanese, Mahnny reached the age of 18 and was therefore eligible to be drafted into the army on a compulsory basis. Fortunately for his family, he was assigned to the Signal Corps stationed nearby. He was often free to spend his nights at home and remained on the Island of Oahu throughout his tour of duty past the end of the war.

Now Song's wife hung a flag with three stars in the bedroom window, an honor not given to many others in the community.

As everyone expected she would, Evelyn eventually married Warren or Hardy Lee, studying at the Moody Bible Institute in Chicago, Illinois. Prior to completion of his studies, he was drafted into the army and was stationed near Joplin, Missouri where his wife was able to find living quarters, just off the base.

Soon, they were blessed with a daughter, whom they called Priscilla. And within two years, Priscilla had a brother, Warren Hardy Lee, Jr.

A bit of sad news reached Song and his wife regarding Evelyn's brother-in-law, a bombadier for the U.S. Airforce in the European theater of war. He was killed after their bomber crashed into the Atlantic Ocean after a successful bombing raid.

Before the end of the conflict with Germany, George completed OCS at Fort Benning, Georgia, graduating in the top fifth in a class of more than 300 candidates. The new Lieutenant Song was assigned to Fort McCuller in Alabama training troops and enlisted sargents in map reading and other activities for ten months. Visits and correspondence with Soo Nam continued and before George was transferred to Fort Monmouth, New Jersey to serve at a German Prisoner of War Camp, he married her. Together, they weathered it to the end of the war, first with Italy and then Germany.

After a seeming eternity, finally, the United States was winning the war in the Pacific. The dropping of the atom bombs at Hiroshima and Nagasaki brought gladness on the one hand, but an eerie sense of unknown fear to Song who wondered if the radioactive effects could reach across the straits to Korea.

As news of the fall and unconditional surrender of Japan was announced, Song and his wefe were filled with gratitude that the awful war was over. However, they began to wonder about the fate of Korea as details were given of the Russians declaring war on Japan on August 8th, 1945 after feelers for an armistice to be effected had been made by the defeated Japanese. By August 12th, the Russians had moved their troops to the 38th parallel of Korea, an ominous happening. There followed a sequence of events that split the nation of Korea into two countries, physically. Chongsong and Pusan were far south of the 38th parallel, but what of the millions of Koreans who would be trapped by the artificial demarcation brought on by the Russian move? Would they be able to freely move across the demarcation line? Would there be a difference in political and living conditions between the two Koreas? Song and his family and the rest of the world wondered. But for now, everyone looked to the benefits of the end to hostilities, never paying a mind to the details, such as the declaration of war by the Russians only days before the unconditional surrender of the Empire of Japan.

Soon thereafter, the war ended with Japan and George had served long enough to be honorably discharged. He left the army and returned home with his bride aboard the U.S.S. Lurline, returning to life free of obligations but to himself and his bride.

POSTWAR CHANGES

With the end of the war, Song felt a need to consolidate his family. George was returning with his new bride and Evelyn promised to return as soon as her husband could effect an honorable discharge. Henry would return before long and Mahnny was stationed near Wahiawa, even coming home several days a week. Soo Sun was about to graduate from high school and Oggie was coming along nicely in junior high school.

He had managed to expand his trade, now operating several shops scattered throughout Schofield Barracks. Despite the shortage of trained craftsmen, he managed to maintain a roster of loyal, hardworking staff to get the job done well. Besides, his two younger daughters were increasingly helpful, pitching in on holidays, vacation periods, and even after school.

Was this a new turning point for him and his wife? Were they to fluorish now that another major obstacle, the war, had been overcome, or had a plateau been reached? Song and his wife were to experience an unprecedented decade of change never imagined by either before. It was not going to take long after the unconditional surrender of the Japanese for the family to regroup in Hawaii, he hoped.

Soon after the return of George with his bride, Evelyn returned with her husband and, not one but two children, Priscilla, a precocious three year old and Warren Hardy, Junior, an infant under a year of age. Then, Henry returned, ready to continue his college education at the University of Hawaii with a major in Prelaw.

George and his bride now occupied the downstairs suite while Evelyn and her husband moved to quarters for military families after her husband had decided to rejoin the army in Hawaii as a Staff Sargeant.

Using the GI Bill of Rights to cover his educational costs, Henry enrolled at the University. There, he subsequently met Betsy Ki Jun Lyum from Honolulu and their meeting soon led to a plan for marriage. This was the first wedding preparation that Suk Soon and his wife had the privilege to prepare. Evelyn and George had married while each was away from home.

Henry and Betsy's wedding was held in Honolulu and the preparations for the wedding feast were to be accomplished by the groom's family, as was the custom in Korea. For days, Bok Pil and her close friends, including the wife of the Reverend Lee, prepared the many different dishes to be served on such an auspicious occasion.

The Reverend Lee had passed away some years earlier. Mrs. Lee had moved to Wahiawa with her daughter and son from Korea plus the two new children born since her arrival in Hawaii. She and Bok Pil had reestablished their close bond and lived as sisters might in any society.

So, the women prepared the chahn-chi (feast) which was transported to the site selected for the reception nearly 25 miles away in Honolulu. The wedding and reception were beautifully accomplished and vignettes were captured on film for distribution amongst the family members.

Sometime thereafter, the issue of the continued leasing of the property at Lehua Street had to be rereviewed. Song had purchased a piece of property on California Avenue in the Heights of Wahiawa, several miles from Lehua Street. It was Song's intent to eventually build a home there inasmuch as the Lightfoots did not appear to want to sell their property over the nearly two decades that he had leased the land. Upon the most recent delivery of a check for his yearly lease, Song was informed that the Lehua Street property was for sale at a price he could not afford just then. Before long, Song was informed that two Japanese farmers had come up with the funds to purchase the entire estate. Song was advised to relinquish his hold and stay on the property within a year.

About this time, Mahnny's two year tour of duty with the Signal Corps was over. He told his father he was willing to use his GI Bill of Rights to obtain a mortgage to build a home for the family. Following up on his promise, Mahnny sought an architect and helped with the drafting of plans for a modern one-story house with a veranda, two baths, three bedrooms, a large living room-dining room area and a substantial eat-in kitchen. The house was completed in about six months and the family moved into a newly built structure for the first time for any of them.

In the meantime, Mahnny had developed an interest in flying, enrolling in a course at the Flying School located at the Honolulu Airport. Not long after, he flew a Piper Cub over the property, buzzing and buzzing as he had forewarned the family that he would. Of course, the family members heard him, running outdoors in the yard to wave at him. Several months later, he received his flying license and he followed this by announcing his interest in pursuing a career as a commercial pilot.

He subsequently left for Tulsa, Oklahoma for training to become a licensed commercial pilot. While away, he married Ella Yong, a lovely Chinese girl he had introduced to the family while they were at Lehua Street. She had flown to be with him in Tulsa.

Once training was completed, he landed a job with a company that flew cargo in and out of various Caribbean Islands and Florida. Mahnny and Ella moved to Florida and in due course were blessed with their first child, Andrea, who was born in Coral Gables, Florida.

With Andrea less than a year of age, they returned to Hawaii when Mahnny had landed a job as a pilot with Aloha Airlines. In time, Mahnny built a home for himself and his family on the upper part of the piece of property his Father had purchased for which Mahnny had obtained the mortgage to build the house for his parents.

Thus, Mahnny and his family occupied the front house while Song, his wife and two younger daughters occupied the second house on the property at 1993 California Avenue in Wahiawa on the Island of Oahu.

Other grandbabies were being born and were growing and maturing rapidly.

Soo Sun was attending the University of Hawaii in premedicine and was soon to graduate. The question arose as to her graduate study in medicine. Hawaii had no medical school, making it incumbent on Soo Sun to go off to the continental U.S. to further her education in medicine. As it was, many GI's were returning with full support of their Bill of Rights who were clogging the educational system, making it highly competitive to gain entry into medical school.

Oggie had already graduated from the newly constructed

Leilehua High School on California Avenue about a mile away from Song's new home. She began working at Song's shops, managing sales and contracts.

In 1950 when Song was 67 and his wife was 54 years of age, Benny Song, an unrelated Korean photographer in Wahiawa, was invited to take a portrait of his growing clan. Everyone dressed and posed for this occasion. A copy of this photograph was framed and hung in Song's home. Viewing it on a daily basis brought such joy to the two immigrants. Each had traveled far in search of a better life and each believed such was accomplished. They happily reminded everyone of the need to regroup for another photograph after the birth of each additional grandchild.

FAMILY PORTRAIT: Included in the photograph, seated to the viewer's left: Evelyn Hae Sun Song Lee, Ella Young Song (Andrew or Mahnny's wife), Ellen Soo Sun Song, Bok Pil Chun Song, Song Suk Soon, Jessie Jea Sun Song, Betsy Lyum Song (Henry or Sung Gun's wife), and Soo Nam Chung Song (Sung Tahn or George's wife). Standing in the back are: Warren Hardy Lee (Evelyn or Hae Sun's husband), Andrew Sung Mahn Song holding daughter Andrea Song, George Joseph Sung Tahn Song, and Henry Sung Gun Song. Children in the front row are: Warren Hardy Lee, Jr., Priscilla Lee, Wesley Lee, Elladene Lee, and Timothy Lee (children of Evelyn and Warren Lee), Barron Song Sim Song and Gayle Song (children of Henry and Betsy Song), Elizabeth Song, and Reuben Song (children of George and Soo Nam Song).

KOREAN WAR AND EVENTS AFTER THE TRUCE

With only a brief respite since the end of World War II, war broke out again on June 25, 1950. North Korea moved with Russian equipment to conquer South Korea on this fateful day. Fortunately for the free world and South Korea, President Harry Truman elected to support the United Nations effort to thwart the communist aggressors.

Both George and Henry were members of the Army Reserves following their tour of duty during World War II. Both were immediately reinducted into the Army. They were sent to the Far East, George to Japan and Henry to Korea. Both were officers and were engaged in either intelligence work or as personnel on the staff of the military leaders of our Army.

Warren or Hardy, Evelyn's husband, continued to serve in the Army at Schofield Barracks until after the three-years of fighting had come to a truce.

In contrast to World War II, knowledge that her sons were not in the front lines helped to keep Bok Pil less agitated and stressed. Both parents kept up with the news and progress of the war, praying for their sons and for the citizens of Korea.

Finally, when a truce was reached and the Korean Conflict ended, both Suk Soon and his wife expected their sons to return home forthwith. Instead, George continued to serve, but was now stationed in Japan. His family was allowed to join him there, where they lived for more than two years.

After the Panmunjon truce was underway and reconstruction of Korea was begun, George invited both of his parents to visit Japan and Korea. His Father agreed to return for a visit to Korea, but his Mother declined to return.

So, George arranged for his Father to visit Chongsong. This was accomplished by contacting his Mother's nephew living in Japan, who was engaged in trade with Korea.

Song traveled to Japan by air. As he looked out of the window, he saw nothing but ripples of blue-grey waters below, reaching far out as far as the horizon. The expanse of Tae-pyung-yang was awesome to him. Imagine, he thought to himself, it took so long to cross this vastness nearly 50 years before and now it would take a little more than half a day!

His head was whirling with thoughts of the past and forebodings of what he might find was left of the home he left so long ago.

He landed in Japan and was met by George and Soo Nam and their family of three children, Reuben, Elizabeth, and baby Milton. He stayed with them, acquainting himself with his grandchildren and renewing his knowledge of colloquial Japanese.

His wife's nephew arrived in Japan and within days Song left Japan with him to visit Korea. They reached Pusan by ferry boat across the straits of Shimonoseki and from Pusan they made their way to Chongsong by train and a hired car.

There in Chongsong, he found his sister's daughter was still alive, living with one of her two sons, both of whom were farmers in the area. He learned that his brother, Suk Chul, had died as did his wife and only son, the one he used to pick up and hoist up in the air. Suk Chul's daughters had left the area having married farmers in other regions of Kyongsang-puk-do.

Song wandered around, barely recognizing the terrain. He searched for and found his parents' burial mounds and paid appropriate obeisances to each. He decided to move their remains to the best sites possible and consulted one of the elders in the community of Chongsong who could divine such sites.

RETURN TO KOREA FOR SONG, after the Korean War

The diviner looked carefully at Song, recalling in his own vague memory the sight of young Suk Soon who was his peer at the activities held by the townspeople gathering for Chusok long, long ago. When the cobwebs were cleared and he had full recall, he broke out in glee and told Song that he was Hyun Minh Chung, his buddy at Chusok when they would race around in the fields as the singing, chanting and feasting went on. Now Song could see images taking shape of Hyun Minh Chung, himself and Lee Yong Soo running the course to beat each other out before they stopped to join in the feasting. They reminisced about the events of their lives that had brought them to this day. Sadly, Song told Hyun of Lee Yong Soo's death.

Finally, Hyun returned to the subject of Song's inquiry, namely, finding the best burial sites for his Mother and Father's remains. Hyun indicated that they were buried at the best sites possible and that their remains should not be moved.

Reassurred, Song prepared a memorial ceremony in honor of his parents. An elaborate feast was prepared to which the people living around his old family farm and those near his nephew's property were invited.

FEAST IN MEMORY OF SONG'S PARENTS

Instead of purchasing sites for his parents' remains, Song used the money he had set aside to purchase additional farmland for each of his two nephews. He was especially careful to equalize the number of pyeongs (unit of property) he purchased, making certain that the younger and the older nephews had an equivalent increase in farmlands. He did not want to see any advantage given or taken away from them on the basis of birth order. It was enough that he had suffered badly from such a custom and he would personally see that any favors he had to offer anyone would never, never take such a form, ever.

After revisiting the landmarks of his life in Korea, Song returned to Japan for a brief stay before flying back to Hawaii. He had come to bring closure to the lingering anger he felt over the meanness of his brother when he was so vulnerable and young. Learning of the demise of that line of Songs, he grieved. He resolved to move forward and release all the vestiges of anger he ever felt. The underlying problem was the unkind law of primogenitor which he had never and would never practice himself. He prayed that such an ancient misjustice would become obsolete and be rejected by everyone, both legally and by custom.

Sadly, he also realized that he would not be returning to the land of his birth again. But he did not wallow in grief and regret. He reviewed the events of his life since his arrival in Hawaii-meeting the woman with the guts to reject a fraudulent sponsor, marrying her and being rewarded with a family of three strong, healthy sons and three wholesome, healthy daughters. He briefly thought of Hae Jun, the son who died before his first birthday, but quickly moved on to think of his growing family of grandchildren. How wonderful it seemed to him to have successfully moved from an ancient farming culture to the challenges offered by life in Hawaii! His children were fully adapted and his grandchildren know nothing of such a difficult life as he had experienced in the Hermit Kingdom. Still, he was filled with love for the Land of the Morning Calm and the memories he would forever hold dear to him-those of his beloved Mother and Honorable Father.

During Song's absence, his wife and Oggie had flown to San Francisco, California to visit Soo Sun, as previously agreed upon. Bok Pil did not have a desire to return to Korea, preferring instead to spend time visiting a small part of the vast expanse of the United States of America, her adopted home.

Soo Sun had gone off to study medicine on the mainland. She had spent the first year at the Woman's Medical College of Pennsylvania in Philadelphia, PA, but transferred to Stanford Medical School in Palo Alto, California in her second year. Medical school classes at Stanford University were held in San Francisco after the first half of the sophomore year. She returned home the summer after her first year of study in Philadelphia, but was unable to return the following summer. So, her Mother and Oggie went to her for a visit.

Their travels included all the touristy spots in and around San Francisco, Lake Tahoe and Yosemite National Park. The trio traveled in a used English Ford which Soo Sun had purchased to ease her travels as a medical student from Lane Hospital to the City and County Hospital in San Francisco, the two clinical facilities used by the medical school.

When Soo Sun asked her Mother why she did not travel to Korea with Father, she replied that she would never return there again, that her destiny was in the United States linked with her childrens' lives. She loved what she saw and had experienced in America, she said. She stipulated that she would seek to become a citizen, not remaining only as a permanent resident.

When both parents returned to Hawaii after their separate

trips, one back to Korea the land of his birth and the other to the continental U.S. the land of promise mostly fulfilled, each was ready to retire and give up the daily struggles at work, resting in the laurels of the work each had already accomplished.

THE END OF THE BEGINNING

As it turned out, Song had been in his own business, not contributing to Social Security for Retirement Benefits for himself. George had arranged for Song to invest in a program to assure him a small pension upon retirement. Evelyn took over the management of the shops and paid a monthly amount to her parents. With this and the sale of their home in Wahiawa, they purchased a less costly home in Kailua, on the windward side of the island of Oahu. Oggie continued to reside with her parents.

This arrangement worked nicely at first, but it wasn't long before the financial restrictions would become too much for Bok Pil, especially.

Soo Sun had her degree in medicine, but elected to seek further training in Pediatrics in Boston, Massachusetts. While there, she met and married a medical student from Seoul, Korea, who was at Harvard Medical School. The family had objected to her marriage fearing the student might be taking advantage of her citizenship status for his own gain. After a brief period of misunderstanding arising from such consideration, communication was re-established and visits were made to enhance mutual acceptance and regard.

Both parents and Oggie traveled together to visit Soo Sun in Boston on one occasion and later in Bethesda, Maryland where Soo Sun's husband landed a Research Fellowship at the National Institute of Health.

They also had a brief stay in Los Angeles, California where they considered the possibility of a permanent move. However, it became clear to both that changes were difficult to make, the environment was unfamiliar and that they missed their community of Korean friends all around them, as it was in Hawaii. Consequently, they returned to Hawaii.

A few years later, Oggie began to work at the Medical Library of Honolulu. There, she met a young lawyer, Don Gelber. Don was of Jewish background and was extremely personable and kind. It wasn't long after that they married.

For Song and his wife, there followed a series of moves with one of their children or the other for variable periods of time. Whereas Song mostly lived with Mahnny and his family, his wife moved from one place to another, seemingly unhappy with her stay with any of her children, but in reality missing her life before retirement and Song's vigor and leadership.

One day at the age of 84, Song was suddenly struck with a pain in the chest. He was hospitalized immediately. A few days later, he appeared to be recovering and everyone was hopeful of his return to his usual activities. Instead unexpectedly a few days later, he died without anyone present at his bedside. Apparently, he suffered a fatal stroke complicating the heart attack.

In reality, he died alone and suddenly so as not to burden anyone with the agony of his last struggle with breathing. After all, he was the Pure or Solid Rock who would leave no pebbles to interfere with anyone's step, but would drop or rise in one piece, solid and unbroken.

At his funeral which was held at the Liliha Korean Christian Church in Honolulu, the hall was packed with people as Koreans and other ethnic friends poured out to bid him farewell. Even though Song no longer lived in Wahiawa, people from that little town drove the 28 miles or so to attend his last rites.

Following the ceremony, he was buried in Nuuanu Cemetery at the age of 84.

Bok Pil could hardly imagine the loss of her husband. She had loved him deeply and selected him personally to be her husband. They had lived an adventurous life together, witnessed their childrens' maturation and their family's expansion. Sure, she was disappointed in a number of things, especially the reduction in their monthly income which infringed on their ability to enjoy their retirement. But, they were cared for and loved by their children.

How would she cope alone? She sorrowed and sorrowed so deeply, finding it difficult to see through her tears, let alone walk down the hall behind his casket without holding on to Oggie.

At the burial site, she could hardly walk to a seat without holding on to Oggie. By the end of the ceremony, it was clear that Bok Pil herself had suffered a stroke.

She was immediately admitted to the hospital. She remained there for many months before she was transferred to a nursing home.

Eleven months after Song's death, his wife followed him to the grave at the age of 72.

Clearly, she had died of a broken heart on the day of mourning and the burial of the very man she herself had selected to be her husband. She could not and would not live without him. She had elected to follow him in death, but the route was a long and hard one for her and the children she left behind.

Thus, the saga of this lineage of Korean immigrants stemming from Song Suk Soon, the patriarch, and his bride, Chun Bok Pil, the matriarch, reached the end of it's first geneological milestone through their passing in 1967 and 1968, respectively.

Each had left Korea, the eastern peninsula of Asia, to seek a better life. Without a promise of such, each sought a way better than they foresaw for themselves under the circumstances of their individual private lives in the land of their birth. Having found each other, they worked together and through their differences to capture the fruits of their hard work.

The land they adopted had granted each a certificate of citizenship, in 1958 for Bok Pil and 1959 for Suk Soon, completing their transition from the Land of the Morning Calm to the Land of the Free. Together they had tried to transplant themselves on the mainland of these United States, but found it better to remain in the middle of Tae-pyung-yang rather than fully across it, before it was too late.

Now, their remains lie side by side in Nuuanu, on the island of Oahu where their children continue to visit them every now and then. The site is in the midst of the cemetery and the cemetery is in the midst of the community of Honolulu-a place where peoples of many nations gather to live and dream of tomorrow and better things to come, without fear.

Their legacy consists of six children who continue to extend their views on the need to seek honorable venues to improve their lives. These views have now been extended to a next generation of children and hopefully will be transmitted in turn to another, perpetuating the dream that Song and Bok Pil grasped before they left the Hermit Kingdom so long ago and far away.